Advancing Maths for AQA
STATISTICS 4

Roger Williamson and Gill Buqué

Series editors
Roger Williamson   Sam Boardman
Ted Graham   Keith Parramore

1 Probability distributions   1

2 Confidence intervals   23

3 Hypothesis testing   45

4 Further hypothesis testing for means   63

5 Contingency tables   83

Exam style practice paper   105

Appendix   108

Answers   112

Index   121

D1427326

Heinemann Educational Publishers
a division of Heinemann Publishers (Oxford) Ltd,
Halley Court, Jordan Hill, Oxford OX2 8EJ

OXFORD JOHANNESBURG BLANTYRE MELBOURNE
AUCKLAND IBADAN GABORONE PORTSMOUTH NH (USA)
CHICAGO

First published in 2001

05   04   03   02
10   9   8   7   6   5   4   3   2

ISBN 0 435 51315 X

Cover design by Miller, Craig and Cocking

Typeset and illustrated by Tech-Set Limited, Gateshead, Tyne & Wear

Printed and bound by Scotprint in the UK

Acknowledgements
The publishers and authors acknowledge the work of the writers, David Cassell,
Ian Hardwick, Mary Rouncefield and David Burghes of the *AEB Mathematics for
AS and A Level* Series, from which some exercises and examples have been
taken.

The authors and publishers would like to thank the BMJ Publishing Group for
permission to use the data on p.102. The data in Q7 p.67 from *The Lancet*
Vol 348, No 9035, 1996 is reprinted with permission from Elsevier Science.

The publishers' and authors' thanks are due to the AQA for permission to
reproduce questions from past examination papers.

The answers have been provided by the authors and are not the responsibility
of the examining board.

About this book

This book is one in a series of textbooks designed to provide you with exceptional preparation for AQA's new Advanced GCE Specification B. The series authors are all senior members of the examining team and have prepared the textbooks specifically to support you in studying this course.

Finding your way around

The following are there to help you find your way around when you are studying and revising:

- **edge marks** (shown on the front page) – these help you to get to the right chapter quickly;
- **contents list** – this identifies the individual sections dealing with key syllabus concepts so that you can go straight to the areas that you are looking for;
- **index** – a number in bold type indicates where to find the main entry for that topic.

Key points

Key points are not only summarised at the end of each chapter but are also boxed and highlighted within the text like this:

> If A and B are two events then A ∪ B or the **union** of A and B is defined as 'A or B' which is the combined event 'at least one of A and B occurs'.

Exercises and exam questions

Worked examples and carefully graded questions familiarise you with the specification and bring you up to exam standard. Each book contains:

- Worked examples and worked exam questions to show you how to tackle typical questions; examiner's tips will also provide guidance;
- Graded exercises, gradually increasing in difficulty up to exam-level questions, which are marked by an [A];
- Test-yourself sections for each chapter so that you can check your understanding of the key aspects of that chapter and identify any sections that you should review;
- Answers to the questions are included at the end of the book.

1 Probability distributions

Learning objectives   1
1.1 Introduction   1
1.2 Expectation of a discrete random variable   1
1.3 Mean and variance of a discrete random variable   2
1.4 Expectation of a continuous random variable   9
1.5 Mean and variance of a continuous random
    variable   10
1.6 The rectangular distribution   15
Key point summary   20
Test yourself   21

2 Confidence intervals

Learning objectives   23
2.1 Introduction   23
2.2 Confidence interval for the mean of a normal
    distribution, standard deviation known   23
2.3 Confidence interval for the mean based on a
    large sample   29
2.4 Confidence interval for the mean of a normal
    distribution, standard deviation unknown   39
Key point summary   43
Test yourself   44

3 Hypothesis testing

Learning objectives   45
3.1 Forming a hypothesis   45
3.2 One- and two-tailed tests   46
3.3 Testing a hypothesis about a population mean   47
3.4 Critical region and significance level of test   47
3.5 General procedure for carrying out a
    hypothesis test   49
3.6 Significance levels and problems to consider   54
3.7 Errors   55
Key point summary   59
Test yourself   61

4 Further hypothesis testing for means

Learning objectives   63
4.1 Hypothesis test for means based on a large
    sample from an unspecified distribution   63

4.2 Hypothesis test for means based on a sample
     from a normal distribution with an unknown
     standard deviation   67
4.3 Mixed examples   73
Key point summary   80
Test yourself   81

5 Contingency tables

Learning objectives   83
5.1 Contingency tables   83
5.2 Small expected values   92
5.3 Yates' correction for 2×2 contingency tables   98
Key point summary   103
Test yourself   104

Exam style practice paper   105

Appendix   108

Table 3 Normal distribution function   108
Table 4 Percentage points of the normal
     distribution   109
Table 5 Percentage points of the student's
     t distribution   110
Table 6 Percentage points of the χ^2-distribution   111

Answers   112

Index   121

CHAPTER I

Probability distributions

Learning objectives

After studying this chapter you should be able to:

■ find the expected value, standard deviation and variance of discrete and continuous random variables

■ use the rectangular distribution.

1.1 Introduction

In book S1 you have already met discrete distributions such as the binomial and Poisson distributions and continuous distributions such as the normal distribution.

It is possible to list the values a **discrete** variable may take together with their associated probabilities. A **continuous** variable may take any value in a range and probability is represented by the area under a curve.

1.2 Expectation of a discrete random variable

The expected value of a discrete random variable, X, is usually denoted $E(X)$.

> A random variable is a variable whose value is (within limits) determined by chance

> The expected value of a discrete random variable X is
>
> $$E(X) = \Sigma x P(X = x)$$

The summation is over all possible values of X.

In the AQA Formulae Book $P(X = x)$ is denoted P_i.

For example if X has the probability distribution below

x	0	2	8	10
$P(X = x)$	0.4	0.3	0.2	0.1

$$E(X) = (0 \times 0.4) + (2 \times 0.3) + (8 \times 0.2) + (10 \times 0.1) = 3.2$$

$E(X)$ is the mean score we would expect to obtain if samples were repeatedly taken from this distribution.

Random variables are usually denoted by an upper case letter such as X. Particular values of a random variable are usually denoted by a lower case letter such as x.

The expectation of g(X), where g(X) is any function of X is given by

$$E[g(X)] = \Sigma g(x)P(X = x)$$

The summation is over all possible values of X.

For example for the distribution above if g(X) = X^2

$$E(X^2) = (0^2 \times 0.4) + (2^2 \times 0.3) + (8^2 \times 0.2) + (10^2 \times 0.1) = 24$$

Note: X is squared **not** the probability.

1.3 Mean and variance of a discrete random variable

The mean of a discrete random variable is defined to be E(X).

This is often denoted by μ.

The mean of X is E(X).

This is the definition of the mean of a random variable and is not the same as the definition of the mean of a set of data. However the two means are closely related.

For a set of data which consists of the observations x_1, x_2,... x_n occuring with frequency f_1, f_2,... f_n respectively, the mean is $\Sigma f_i x_i / \Sigma f_i$. This may be written $\Sigma x_i(f_i/\Sigma f_i)$. The definition of the mean of a probability distribution is obtained by replacing the relative frequency of occurrence of x_i, ($f_i/\Sigma f_i$), by the probability of x_i.

For a similar reason the variance of a discrete random variable is defined to be $E[\{X - E(X)\}^2]$.

This is often denoted by σ^2.

The variance of a discrete random variable is defined

$$\mathbf{Var}(X) = E[\{X - E(X)\}^2]$$

For the distribution above we have calculated E(X), the mean, as 3.2

x	0	2	8	10
$(x - 3.2)^2$	10.24	1.44	23.04	46.24
$P(X = x)$	0.4	0.3	0.2	0.1

Here g(X) = $(X - 3.2)^2$.

The variance of X

$$\begin{aligned} Var(X) &= (10.24 \times 0.4) + (1.44 \times 0.3) \\ &\quad + (23.04 \times 0.2) + (46.24 \times 0.1) \\ &= 13.76 \end{aligned}$$

It is straightforward to show algebraically that

$$E[\{X - E(X)\}^2] = E(X^2) - [E(X)]^2$$

You will not be asked to prove this.

Or $\sigma^2 = E(X^2) - \mu^2$.

This is an easier way of calculating the variance. We have already calculated $E(X) = 3.2$ and $E(X^2) = 24$.
Thus, $\mathrm{Var}(X) = 24 - 3.2^2 = 13.76$ as before.

The variance plays an important role in mathematical statistics but the standard deviation is a more natural measure of spread. This is found by simply taking the square root of the variance.

In this case standard deviation $= \sqrt{13.76} = 3.71$.

Worked example 1.1

In a 'pay and display' car park, motorists use an automatic machine to purchase tickets. The price, $£X$, of the ticket depends on the length of time the motorist intends to leave the car. The following probability distribution provides a suitable model for the random variable X.

x	$P(X = x)$
0.8	0.25
1.4	0.55
2.0	0.08
2.8	p

(a) Find the value of p.
(b) Calculate the mean and the standard deviation of X.
(c) A few motorists park but do not purchase a ticket. It is decided to modify the probability distribution to include these motorists by allocating a small probability to the outcome $X = 0$. Will the standard deviation of the modified probability distribution be greater, the same or smaller than that calculated in (b)?

Solution

(a) $p = 1 - 0.25 - 0.55 - 0.08 = 0.12$

(b) $E(X) = (0.8 \times 0.25) + (1.4 \times 0.55) + (2.0 \times 0.08)$
$\qquad\qquad + (2.8 \times 0.12)$
$\qquad = 1.466$

$E(X^2) = (0.8^2 \times 0.25) + (1.4^2 \times 0.55) + (2.0^2 \times 0.08)$
$\qquad\qquad + (2.8^2 \times 0.12)$
$\qquad = 2.4988$

variance of $X = 2.4988 - 1.466^2 = 0.3496$
standard deviation $= \sqrt{0.3496} = 0.591$

(c) If $X = 0$ is included in the probability distribution it will be more spread out and so the standard deviation will be increased.

The sum of all the probabilities must equal one.

Don't round to 3 sf at this stage. You will need to keep all these figures in order to obtain the standard deviation correct to 3 sf.

Worked example 1.2

A newsagent sells phone cards valued at £1, £2, £4, £10 and £20. The value, in £, of a phone card sold may be regarded as a random variable, X, with the following probability distribution:

x	$P(X = x)$
1	0.20
2	0.40
4	0.22
10	0.11
20	0.07

(a) Find the mean and standard deviation of X.

(b) What is the probability that the value of the next phone card sold is less than £4?

The newsagent is considering whether to discontinue selling £1 and £2 cards. If she did this a proportion, p, of customers who presently buy £1 or £2 cards would then buy a £4 card. Other such customers would not buy a card. As a result the value, in £, of sales would be a random variable, Y, with the following probability distribution:

y	$P(Y = y)$
0	$0.6(1 - p)$
4	$0.22 + 0.6p$
10	0.11
20	0.07

(c) Find the mean of Y in terms of p.

A survey suggests that the value of p would be between 0.5 and 0.7.

(d) Using this information, advise the newsagent on the likely effect on takings if she decides to discontinue selling £1 and £2 cards. Also point out factors, other than receipts from phone cards, which she should consider before making a decision. [A]

Solution

(a) $E(X) = (1 \times 0.2) + (2 \times 0.4) + (4 \times 0.22) + (10 \times 0.11) + (20 \times 0.07)$
   $= £4.38$

   $E(X^2) = (1^2 \times 0.2) + (2^2 \times 0.4) + (4^2 \times 0.22) + (10^2 \times 0.11)$
   $+ (20^2 \times 0.07) = 44.32$

   > Don't forget to square X, **not** the probability.

   $\text{variance} = 44.32 - 4.38^2 = 25.1356$
   $\text{standard deviation} = \sqrt{25.1356} = £5.01$

(b) Probability less than £4 $= 0.20 + 0.40 = 0.60$

(c) $E(Y) = (0 \times 0.6(1 - p)) + 4(0.22 + 0.6p) + (10 \times 0.11) + (20 \times 0.07)$
   $= £(3.38 + 2.4p)$

(d) The survey suggests that p will be 0.5 or higher. The expected takings will be £4.58 or higher. Thus there will be an increase in takings from phone cards. However there may be a loss of goodwill and some customers who used to buy £1 and £2 phone cards may no longer come into the shop. This could lead to a reduction in the sales of other items.

Worked example 1.3

The four directors of a company each have a parking space reserved for them at head office. Based on past observations, the number of these spaces occupied at 10.00 a.m. on a weekday morning may be modelled by a random variable, R, with the following probability distribution:

r	0	1	2	3	4
$P(R = r)$	0.25	0.30	0.15	0.10	0.20

(a) Calculate the mean and standard deviation of R.

(b) It is suggested that a binomial distribution may provide an adequate model for R. Assuming that this is correct:

   (i) use the mean you have calculated in **(a)** to estimate p, the probability that a parking space is occupied at 10.00 a.m. on a weekday morning,

   (ii) use your estimate of p to estimate the standard deviation of R.

(c) Do your calculations support the suggestion that a binomial distribution provides an adequate model for R?

(d) Give two reasons why, irrespective of your calculations, a binomial distribution may not be an appropriate model for R.   [A]

Solution

(a) $E(R) = (0 \times 0.25) + (1 \times 0.30) + (2 \times 0.15) + (3 \times 0.10) + (4 \times 0.20)$
$$= 1.7$$
$E(R^2) = (0^2 \times 0.25) + (1^2 \times 0.30) + (2^2 \times 0.15) + (3^2 \times 0.10) + (4^2 \times 0.20)$
$$= 5.0$$

variance of $R = 5 - 1.7^2 = 2.11$
standard deviation $= \sqrt{2.11} = 1.45$

(b) **(i)** Mean of binomial is np. In this case the mean $= 1.7$ and $n = 4$ hence estimate of

$$p = \frac{1.7}{4} = 0.425$$

   (ii) Standard deviation of binomial is $\sqrt{np(1 - p)}$.

Hence estimated standard deviation of R is $\sqrt{4 \times 0.425(1 - 0.425)} = 0.989$.

(c) The standard deviation calculated from the probability distribution is 1.45. This is not close to 0.989, the estimate based on assuming a binomial distribution. Hence calculations suggest that binomial is not an adequate model.

(d) p may not be constant. Different directors may have different probabilities of using car parking space at 10.00 a.m.

Use of car parking space may not be independent. A meeting on the premises may mean that all directors will be using their parking spaces whereas a meeting off the premises may mean that none of the directors will be using their parking spaces.

EXERCISE 1A

1 A discrete random variable, X, has probability distribution defined by

x	0	1	2	3
$P(X = x)$	0.4	0.3	0.2	0.1

Find the mean, variance and standard deviation of X.

2 A discrete random variable, X, has probability distribution defined by

x	0	1	4	10
$P(X = x)$	0.2	0.5	0.2	0.1

Find the mean, variance and standard deviation of X.

3 A discrete random variable, X, has probability distribution defined by

x	0	1	2	3	4
$P(X = x)$	0.2	0.4	0.2	0.1	p

(a) Find p.

(b) Find the mean, variance and standard deviation of X.

4 Members of a public library may borrow up to four books at any one time. The number of books borrowed by a member on each visit to the library is a random variable, X, with the following probability distribution:

x	$P(X = x)$
0	0.24
1	0.12
2	0.20
3	0.28
4	0.16

Find the mean and the standard deviation of X.

5 A regular customer at a small clothes shop observes that the number of customers, X, in the shop when she enters has the following probability distribution:

Number of customers, x	$P(X = x)$
0	0.15
1	0.34
2	0.27
3	0.14
4	0.10

(a) Find the mean and standard deviation of X.

She also observes that the average waiting time, Y, before being served is as follows:

Number of customers, x	Average waiting time, y minutes
0	0
1	2
2	6
3	9
4	12

(b) Find her mean waiting time.

6 Prospective recruits to a large retailing organisation undergo a medical examination. As part of the examination, their heights are measured by a nurse, and recorded to the nearest 2 mm. The final digit of the recorded height may be modelled by a random variable, X, with the following probability distribution:

x	0	2	4	6	8
$P(X = x)$	0.2	0.2	0.2	0.2	0.2

(a) Find the mean and standard deviation of X.

(b) A new nurse recorded the heights to the nearest 5 mm. Construct an appropriate probability distribution for the final digit of the recorded height. [A]

7 A company produces blue carpet material. The length of material (in metres) required to meet each order is a discrete random variable, X, with the following probability distribution:

x	$P(X = x)$
50	0.50
60	0.08
70	0.04
80	0.05
90	0.08
100	0.25

(a) Find the mean and the standard deviation of X.

(b) What is the probability that in a day during which exactly two orders are placed the total length of material ordered is 120 m? [A]

8 Applicants for a sales job are tested on their knowledge of consumer protection legislation. The test consists of five multiple choice questions. The number of correct answers, X, follows the distribution below.

X	0	1	2	3	4	5
$P(X = x)$	0.60	0.04	0.07	0.10	0.09	0.10

(a) Find the mean and standard deviation of X.

A group of production staff, who had no knowledge of the subject, guessed all the answers. The probability of each answer being correct was 0.25. The random variable, Y, represents the distribution of the number of correct answers for this group.

(b) (i) Name the probability distribution which could provide a suitable model for Y.

(ii) Determine the mean and standard deviation of Y.

(c) Compare and comment briefly on the results of your calculations in **(a)** and **(b)(ii)**. [A]

9 A petrol station in a remote area installs a self-service machine which delivers petrol on the insertion of £1 coins. This enables petrol to be obtained when the owner is not available. Observation suggests that the distribution of the value of petrol bought from the machine by each customer is as follows:

Value of petrol, £x	Probability
1	0.18
2	0.12
3	0.22
4	0.18
5	0.12
6	0.08
7	0.06
8	0.04

(a) Find the mean and standard deviation of X.

(b) The owner considers having the machine adjusted so that at least five £1 coins would have to be inserted to obtain petrol. Assume that the distribution of sales to present customers after a change would be as follows:

Value of petrol, £y	Probability
0	$0.7(1 - p)$
5	$0.12 + 0.7p$
6	0.08
7	0.06
8	0.04

Find the mean of Y in terms of p and hence the range of values of p which would lead to an increase in mean sales. [A]

1.4 Expectation of a continuous random variable

The expected value of a continuous random variable, X, is defined to be

$$E(X) = \int x f(x) \, dx$$

> Compared to a discrete distribution Σ has been replaced by $\int$ and $P(X = x)$ has been replaced by $f(x)$.

where $f(x)$ is the probability density function and the range of integration is the range of values for which $f(x)$ is defined.

For example, if the random variable, X, has the probability density function

$$f(x) = \begin{cases} 0.02x & 0 < x < 10 \\ 0 & \text{otherwise} \end{cases}$$

> As this is a continuous distribution it makes no difference whether the range is $0 < x < 10$ or $0 \leqslant x \leqslant 10$.

$$E(X) = \int_0^{10} 0.02x^2 \, dx = \left[\frac{0.02x^3}{3} \right]_0^{10} = 6.67$$

$E(X)$ is the mean score we would expect to obtain if samples were repeatedly taken from this distribution.

The expectation of $g(X)$, where $g(X)$ is any function of X, is given by

$$E[g(X)] = \int g(x) f(x) \, dx$$

> The integration is over the range of values for which x is defined.

For the distribution above

$$E(X^2) = \int_0^{10} 0.02x^3 \, dx = \left[\frac{0.02x^4}{4} \right]_0^{10} = 50$$

> Here $g(X) = X^2$.

1.5 Mean and variance of a continuous random variable

The mean of a continuous distribution is defined to be E(X).
The variance of a continuous distribution is defined to be
$E[\{X - E(X)\}^2]$.
Hence for both discrete and continuous distributions

> **The mean of X is E(X)**
> **The variance of X, Var(X) = $E[\{X - E(X)\}^2]$**
> $\qquad\qquad\qquad\qquad\quad = E(X^2) - [E(X)]^2$

Or $\sigma^2 = E(X^2) - \mu^2$.

As with discrete distributions it is easier to calculate the variance using

$$E[\{X - E(X)\}^2] = E(X^2) - [E(X)]^2$$

For the distribution

$$f(x) = \begin{cases} 0.02x & 0 < x < 10 \\ 0 & \text{otherwise} \end{cases}$$

we have already seen that E(X) = 6.67 and E(X^2) = 50.
Hence the variance is $50 - 6.66667^2 = 5.55556$
and the standard deviation = $\sqrt{5.55556} = 2.36$.

Worked example 1.4

A continuous random variable, X, has probability density function

$$f(x) = \begin{cases} kx & 1 < x < 3 \\ 0 & \text{otherwise} \end{cases}$$

where k is a constant.

(a) Find the value of k.

(b) Find the expectation and standard deviation of X.

Solution

(a) $\qquad \int_1^3 kx\, dx = 1$

The total area under the curve must equal one.

$$k\left[\frac{x^2}{2}\right]_1^3 = 1$$

$$k(4.5 - 0.5) = 1$$

$$k = 0.25$$

(b)
$$E(X) = \int_1^3 0.25x^2 \, dx = \left[\frac{0.25x^3}{3} \right]_1^3$$

$$= 0.25\left(9 - \frac{1}{3} \right)$$

$$= 2.17$$

> The answer is given to 3 sf, but note that it is necessary to use more than 3 sf for E(X) when calculating Var(X).

$$E(X^2) = \int_1^3 0.25x^3 \, dx = \left[\frac{0.25x^4}{4} \right]_1^3 = \frac{81}{16} - \frac{1}{16} = 5$$

$$\mathrm{Var}(X) = 5 - 2.16667^2 = 0.3056$$

$$\text{standard deviation} = \sqrt{0.3056} = 0.553$$

Worked example 1.5

A small shopkeeper sells paraffin. She finds that during the winter the daily demand in gallons, X, may be regarded as a random variable with probability density function

$$f(x) = \begin{cases} kx^2(10 - x) & 0 < x < 10 \\ 0 & \text{otherwise} \end{cases}$$

(a) Verify that k = 0.0012.

(b) Find the arithmetic mean and the standard deviation of the distribution.

(c) $f(x)$ is a maximum when $x = \frac{20}{3}$. What is this value called?

(d) Estimate the median using the approximate relationship

$$2(\text{median} - \text{mean}) = \text{mode} - \text{median}.$$

Verify that your answer is approximately correct by finding the probability that an observation is less than your estimate of the median. [A]

> For a continuous distribution the probability of a random observation being less than the median is 0.5.

Solution

(a)
$$\int_0^{10} kx^2 (10 - x) \, dx = 1$$

$$k\left[\frac{10x^3}{3} - \frac{x^4}{4} \right]_0^{10} = 1$$

$$k\left(\frac{10\,000}{3} - \frac{10\,000}{4} \right) = 1$$

$$k = \frac{1}{833.333} = 0.0012$$

(b)
$$\mathrm{E}(X) = \int_0^{10} 0.0012x^3(10 - x)\,\mathrm{d}x$$

$$= 0.0012\left[\frac{10x^4}{4} - \frac{x^5}{5}\right]_0^{10}$$

$$= 6$$

$$\mathrm{E}(X^2) = \int_0^{10} 0.0012x^4(10 - x)\,\mathrm{d}x$$

$$= 0.0012\left[\frac{10x^5}{5} - \frac{x^6}{6}\right]_0^{10}$$

$$= 40$$

$$\mathrm{Var}(X) = 40 - 6^2 = 4$$
$$\text{standard deviation} = \sqrt{4} = 2$$

(c) f(x) is a maximum at the mode.

(d) estimate median by

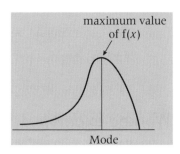
maximum value of f(x)

Mode

$$2(\text{median} - 6) = \frac{20}{3} - \text{median}$$

$$2\,\text{median} - 12 = \frac{20}{3} - \text{median}$$

$$3\,\text{median} = 12 + \frac{20}{3} = \frac{56}{3}$$

$$\text{median} = \frac{56}{9} = 6.22$$

Probability observation less than $6.22 = \int_0^{6.22} 0.0012x^2(10 - x)\,\mathrm{d}x$

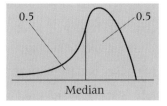
0.5   0.5

Median

$$= 0.0012\left[\frac{10x^3}{3} - \frac{x^4}{4}\right]_0^{6.22}$$

$$= 0.514$$

Hence 6.22 is approximately the median as this probability is close to 0.5.

Worked example 1.6

A charity group raises funds by collecting waste paper. A full skip will contain an amount, X, of other materials such as plastic bags and rubber bands. X may be regarded as a random variable with probability density function

$$f(x) = \begin{cases} \dfrac{2}{9}(x - 1)(4 - x) & 1 < x < 4 \\ 0 & \text{otherwise} \end{cases}$$

(All numerical values in this question are in units of 100 kg)

(a) Find the mean and standard deviation of X.

(b) Find the probability that X exceeds 3.5.

A full skip may normally be sold for £250 but if X exceeds 3.5 only £125 will be paid.

(c) Find the expected value of a full skip.

Alternatively the paper may be sorted before being placed in the skip. This will ensure a very low value of X and a full skip may then be sold for £310. However the effort put into sorting means that 25 per cent fewer full skips will be sold.

(d) Advise the charity whether or not to sort the paper.

Solution

(a) Mean, $E(X) = \int_1^4 \frac{2}{9}x(x-1)(4-x)\,dx$

$$= \frac{2}{9}\int_1^4 (-x^3 + 5x^2 - 4x)\,dx$$

$$= \frac{2}{9}\left[\frac{-x^4}{4} + \frac{5x^3}{3} - \frac{4x^2}{2}\right]_1^4$$

$$= 2.5$$

$$E(X^2) = \frac{2}{9}\int_1^4 (-x^4 + 5x^3 - 4x^2)\,dx$$

$$= \frac{2}{9}\left[\frac{-x^5}{5} + \frac{5x^4}{4} - \frac{4x^3}{3}\right]_1^4$$

$$= 6.7$$

$$\text{variance} = 6.7 - 2.5^2 = 0.45$$
$$\text{standard deviation} = \sqrt{0.45} = 0.671$$

(b) Probability X exceeds 3.5 $= \frac{2}{9}\int_{3.5}^4 (-x^2 + 5x - 4)\,dx$

$$= \frac{2}{9}\left[\frac{-x^3}{3} + \frac{5x^2}{2} - 4x\right]_{3.5}^4$$

$$= 0.0741$$

(c) Expected value of a full skip is
£125 × 0.0741 + £250 × (1 − 0.0741) = £241

(d) If skips are sorted only three-quarters of the number of skips would be sold at £310.
0.75 × £310 = £232.50 which is less than £241. Hence in the long run the charity will make more money if the paper is not sorted.

EXERCISE 1B

1 A continuous random variable, X, has probability density function given by

$$f(x) = \begin{cases} kx & 1 < x < 2 \\ 0 & \text{otherwise} \end{cases}$$

where k is a constant.

(a) Find the value of k.

(b) Find the expected value, the variance and the standard deviation of X.

2 A continuous random variable, X, has probability density function given by

$$f(x) = \begin{cases} 0.048x(5-x) & 0 < x < 5 \\ 0 & \text{elsewhere} \end{cases}$$

Find the mean and the standard deviation of X.

3 A continuous random variable, X, has probability density function

$$f(x) = \begin{cases} 0.375x^2 & 0 < x < 2 \\ 0 & \text{otherwise} \end{cases}$$

Find:
(a) the mean and the standard deviation of X,
(b) the probability that X is less than the mean.

4 A continuous random variable, X, has probability density function

$$f(x) = \begin{cases} 0.15x(x+2) & 0 < x < 2 \\ 0 & \text{elsewhere} \end{cases}$$

Find:
(a) the mean and the standard deviation of X,
(b) the probability X is less than 1.

5 A temporary roundabout is installed at a crossroads. The time, X minutes, which vehicles have to wait before entering the crossroads has probability density function

$$f(x) = \begin{cases} 0.8 - 0.32x & 0 < x < 2.5 \\ 0 & \text{otherwise} \end{cases}$$

Find the mean and standard deviation of X.

6 The random variable, Y, has probability density function

$$f(y) = \begin{cases} k(8 - 2y) & 0 < y < 4 \\ 0 & \text{otherwise} \end{cases}$$

(a) Verify that $k = 0.0625$ and that the median is approximately 1.172.
(b) Find the mean and the standard deviation of Y.
(c) Find the probability that the mean of a random sample of size 50 from this distribution lies between the mean and the median. [A]

7 In an extraction process, an ingredient can be obtained from raw material by one of two methods, P or Q. For a fixed volume of raw material, the amount, $X \, \text{cm}^3$, of ingredient extracted by method P is normally distributed with mean 10 and standard deviation 2. The amount, $Y \, \text{cm}^3$, extracted from the same volume of raw material using method Q is distributed with probability density function

$$f(y) = \begin{cases} k(y - 8) & 8 < y < 12 \\ 0 & \text{otherwise} \end{cases}$$

(a) Find the value of k.

(b) Show that method Q has the greater probability of extracting more than 11 cm³ of the ingredient.

(c) Find which method extracts, on average, the greater amount of the ingredient.

The cost of applying method P is 6p per cm³ extracted and the cost of extracting Y cm³ using method Q is $(15 + 5Y)$p. The extracted ingredient is sold at 10p per cm³.

(d) For a fixed volume of raw material show that method P gives the higher expected profit. [A]

> The pure mathematics required for this question is more complicated than will be needed in the examination.

1.6 The rectangular distribution

So far the only continuous distribution you have met which has a name is the normal distribution. A second continuous distribution which has a name is the rectangular (or uniform) distribution. It is clear from the diagram how this distribution got its name. The probability density function in its most general form is

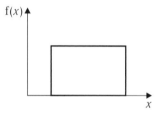

$$f(x) = \begin{cases} \dfrac{1}{(b-a)} & a < x < b \\ 0 & \text{otherwise} \end{cases} \quad \text{where } a \text{ and } b \text{ are constants}$$

$$E(X) = \int_a^b \frac{x}{(b-a)} \, dx = \left[\frac{x^2}{2(b-a)} \right]_a^b$$

$$= \frac{(b^2 - a^2)}{2(b-a)} = \frac{(a+b)}{2}$$

> This algebra is more difficult than anything you are likely to meet in an examination.

$$E(X^2) = \int_a^b \frac{x^2}{(b-a)} \, dx = \left[\frac{x^3}{3(b-a)} \right]_a^b = \frac{(b^3 - a^3)}{3(b-a)}$$

$$\text{Var}(X) = \frac{(b^3 - a^3)}{3(b-a)} - \frac{(a+b)^2}{2^2} = \frac{(b-a)^2}{12}$$

$$E(X) = \frac{(a+b)}{2}$$

$$\text{Var}(X) = \frac{(b-a)^2}{12}$$

> These results are given in the AQA Formulae Book.

Worked example 1.7

Heights of children are measured to the nearest centimetre. The rounding error may be regarded as a random variable, X, with probability density function

$$f(x) = \begin{cases} 1 & -0.5 < x < 0.5 \\ 0 & \text{elsewhere} \end{cases}$$

(a) Find the mean and standard deviation of X.

(b) Show that, for a particular measurement, the probability that the magnitude of the rounding error is less than 0.05 cm is 0.1.

(c) Find, approximately, the probability that, for a random sample of 100 measurements, the magnitude of the mean rounding error is less than 0.05 cm.

Solution

(a) $$E(X) = \int_{-0.5}^{0.5} x \, dx$$

$$= \left[\frac{x^2}{2} \right]_{-0.5}^{0.5}$$

$$= 0.125 - 0.125 = 0$$

$$E(X^2) = \int_{-0.5}^{0.5} x^2 \, dx$$

$$= \left[\frac{x^3}{3} \right]_{-0.5}^{0.5}$$

$$= \frac{0.125}{3} - \left(\frac{-0.125}{3} \right) = 0.08333$$

> Alternatively substitute $a = -0.5$ and $b = 0.5$ into the formulae on page 15.

$$Var(X) = 0.08333 - 0^2 = 0.0833$$

$$\text{standard deviation} = \sqrt{0.08333} \quad = 0.289$$

(b) Probability magnitude of rounding error less than 0.05

$$= \int_{-0.05}^{0.05} 1 \, dx = \left[x \right]_{-0.05}^{0.05}$$

$$= 0.05 - (-0.05) = 0.1$$

(c) The mean of a random sample of 100 will be approximately normally distributed with mean 0 and standard deviation

> See S1 section 7.11.

$$\frac{0.289}{\sqrt{100}} = 0.0289$$

$$z_1 = \frac{0.05 - 0}{0.0289} = 1.732$$

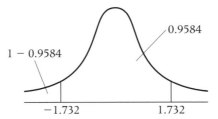

$$z_2 = \frac{-0.05 - 0}{0.0289} = -1.732$$

probability mean rounding error less than 0.05

$$0.9584 - (1 - 0.9584) = 0.917$$

EXERCISE IC

1 A random variable, X, has probability density function defined by

$$f(x) = \begin{cases} k & 4 < x < 9, \quad \text{where k is a constant} \\ 0 & \text{elsewhere} \end{cases}$$

Find:

(a) k,

(b) the mean and variance of X,

(c) the standard deviation of X.

2 A random variable, X, has probability density function

$$f(x) = \begin{cases} k & 0 < x < 10, \quad \text{where k is a constant} \\ 0 & \text{elsewhere} \end{cases}$$

Find:

(a) k,

(b) $P(X = 4)$,

(c) $P(4 < X < 7)$,

(d) the mean and standard deviation of this distribution.

3 A continuous random variable, X, has probability density function

$$f(x) = \begin{cases} k & -1 < x < 4 \\ 0 & \text{otherwise} \end{cases}$$

Find:

(a) k,

(b) $P(X = 0)$,

(c) $P(0 < X < 1)$,

(d) the mean, variance and standard deviation of X.

4 A technique for measuring the density of a silicon compound results in an error which may be modelled by the random variable, X, with probability density function

$$f(x) = \begin{cases} k & -0.04 < x < 0.04 \\ 0 & \text{otherwise} \end{cases}$$

Find:

(a) the value of k,

(b) the mean and standard deviation of X,

(c) the probability that the error is between -0.03 and 0.01,

(d) the probability that the magnitude of the error is greater than 0.035.

5 The error, in grams, made by a greengrocer's scales may be modelled by the random variable, X, with probability density function

$$f(x) = \begin{cases} 0.1 & -3 < x < 7 \\ 0 & \text{otherwise} \end{cases}$$

Find the probability that:

(a) an error is positive,

(b) the magnitude of an error exceeds 2 g (i.e. $|X| > 2$),

(c) the magnitude of an error is less than 4 g (i.e. $|X| < 4$).

MIXED EXERCISE

1 A clothing factory uses rolls of cloth for making suits. The length, in centimetres, of cloth wasted (because it is too short to use) at the end of each roll may be regarded as a random variable, X, with probability density function

$$f(x) = \begin{cases} \dfrac{1}{a} & 0 < x < a \\ 0 & \text{otherwise} \end{cases}$$

(a) Derive the mean, μ, and standard deviation, σ, in terms of a.

(b) Write down the mean and standard deviation of X, the mean of a sample of size n from the distribution.

(c) The median, Y, of a random sample of size three from the distribution has a probability density function

$$f(y) = \begin{cases} \dfrac{6y}{a^2} - \dfrac{6y^2}{a^3} & 0 < y < a \\ 0 & \text{otherwise} \end{cases}$$

Find the mean and variance of Y. [A]

2 Observations on the number of cars, X, passing a fixed point on a road in a minute suggested it could be modelled by the following probability distribution:

x	0	1	2	3	4	5
$P(X = x)$	0.30	0.35	0.24	0.09	0.01	0.01

(a) Find the mean and standard deviation of X.

(b) (i) Name the probability distribution that could provide a suitable model for X.

(ii) If X followed the distribution you have named in (i) with mean 1.19 evaluate the standard deviation of X.

(c) Comment briefly on the results of your calculations in (a) and (b)(ii). [A]

3 In an attempt to economise on her telephone bill, Debbie times her calls and ensures that they never last longer than four minutes. The length of the calls, T, minutes, may be regarded as a random variable with probability density function

$$f(t) = \begin{cases} kt & 0 < t < 4 \\ 0 & \text{otherwise} \end{cases}$$

where k is a constant.

(a) (i) Show that k = 0.125.
(ii) Find the mean and standard deviation of T.
(iii) Find the probability that a call lasts between three and four minutes.

Calls are charged at a rate of 6p per call plus 4p for each complete minute that the call lasts.

(b) (i) Copy and complete the following table.

Length of call, mins	Probability	Cost, pence
0–1		
1–2		
2–3		
3–4		18

(ii) Find the mean and standard deviation of the cost, in pence, of a call. [A]

4 The overall mark obtained by a ski jumper is based on the distance, X m, jumped in excess of 80 m and marks for style, Y.

(a) Assuming that X is a continuous random variable with probability density function

$$f(x) = \begin{cases} ax & 0 < x < 10 \\ 0 & \text{elsewhere} \end{cases}$$

and that Y is a discrete random variable which takes the value y with probability

$$cy \qquad y = 1, 2, 3, 4, 5$$

find a and c.

(b) Evaluate:
(i) the expected distance jumped in excess of 80 m,
(ii) the expected style marks obtained by the ski jumper,
(iii) the expected overall mark for the ski jumper if the total mark, T, is given by

$$T = X^2 + 0.5Y.$$

Note:
$E(T) = E(X^2) + E(0.5Y)$

(c) Assuming X and Y are independent, determine the probability that the ski jumper exceeds 85 m and obtains more than three style marks for a particular jump. [A]

5 A retired couple, living in a country area, supplement their income by providing bed and breakfast for guests. At breakfast guests help themselves to orange juice. The amount, Y l, taken by each guest may be regarded as a random variable with probability density function

$$f(y) = \begin{cases} \dfrac{1000}{33}(y - 2y^2) & 0.1 < y < 0.4 \\ 0 & \text{elsewhere} \end{cases}$$

(a) Evaluate the mean and standard deviation of Y. You may assume that $E(Y^2) = 0.06918$.

(b) Show that the probability that a guest takes less than 0.2 l of orange juice is 0.313 (to three significant figures).

The number of guests staying on a particular night during the summer months may be regarded as a random variable X with the following probability distribution:

x	P(X = x)
0	0.1
1	0.2
2	0.4
3	0.3

The amount of orange juice taken by each guest is independent of the amount taken by other guests.

(c) What is the largest total amount of orange juice that could be taken by the guests on a particular morning?

(d) Given that on a particular night there were three guests, what is the probability that each one took less than 0.2 l?

(e) What is the probability that on a particular night there were three guests and each one took less than 0.2 l?

(f) What is the probability that on a particular night each guest took less than 0.2 l? (Include the possibility that there were no guests that particular night.) [A]

Key point summary

1 For a discrete random variable, X, *p1*

$$E(X) = \Sigma x P(X = x)$$

where the summation is over all possible values of X.

2 For a discrete random variable X, *p2*

$$E[g(X)] = \Sigma g(x) P(X = x)$$

where the summation is over all possible values of X.

3 For a continuous random variable, X,   *p9*

$$E(X) = \int x f(x)\, dx$$

where $f(x)$ is the probability density function and the range of integration is the range of values for which $f(x)$ is defined.

$$E[g(X)] = \int g(x) f(x)\, dx$$

4 The mean of X is $E(X)$ *p10*

5 The variance of X,   *p10*

$$Var(X) = E[\{X - E(X)\}^2] = E(X^2) - [E(X)]^2$$

6 The standard deviation of X is the square root of the variance.   *p10*

7 The probability density function of a rectangular distribution is of the form,   *p15*

$$f(x) = \begin{cases} \dfrac{1}{(b-a)} & a < x < b \\ 0 & \text{otherwise} \end{cases} \quad \begin{array}{l} \text{where a and b} \\ \text{are constants} \end{array}$$

$$E(X) = \frac{(a+b)}{2}$$

$$Var(X) = \frac{(b-a)^2}{12}$$

Test yourself	What to review

1 A discrete random variable, X, has probability density function defined by   *Section 1.3*

X	0	1	4	10
$P(X = x)$	p	$4p$	0.2	0.1

(a) Find p.
(b) Find the probability X is greater than 0.5.

2 A continuous random variable, Y, has probability density function   *Section 1.5*

$$f(y) = \begin{cases} ky^2 & 0 < y < 2 \\ 0 & \text{otherwise} \end{cases}$$

Find k.

Test yourself (*continued*)	What to review

3 A continuous random variable, X, has probability density function

$$f(x) = \begin{cases} 0.2 & -1 < x < 4 \\ 0 & \text{otherwise} \end{cases}$$

Section 1.6

Find:
(a) $P(-1 < X < 2)$,
(b) the mean, variance and standard deviation of X.

4 A continuous random variable, X, has probability density function given by

$$f(x) = \begin{cases} 0.5x & 0 < x < b \\ 0 & \text{otherwise} \end{cases}$$

Section 1.6

Find b.

5 A discrete random variable, R, has probability density function defined by

Section 1.3

r	0.0	0.5	1.0	3.5
$P(R = r)$	0.3	0.4	0.2	0.1

Find the mean, variance and standard deviation of R.

6 A continuous random variable, X, has probability density function given by

$$f(x) = \begin{cases} 0.005x & 0 < x < 20 \\ 0 & \text{otherwise} \end{cases}$$

Section 1.5

Find the mean, the variance and the standard deviation of X.

Test yourself **ANSWERS**

6 13.3, 22.2, 4.71.

5 0.75, 0.9625, 0.981.

4 2.

3 (a) 0.6; (b) 1.5, 2.08, 1.44.

2 0.375.

1 (a) 0.14; (b) 0.86.

CHAPTER 2

Confidence intervals

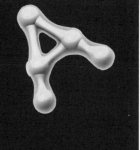

Learning objectives

After reading this chapter you should be able to:

■ calculate a confidence interval for the mean of a normal distribution with a known standard deviation
■ calculate a confidence interval for the mean of any distribution from a large sample
■ calculate a confidence interval for the mean of a normal distribution using the t distribution.

2.1 Introduction

Applying statistics often involves using a sample to draw conclusions about a population. This is known as statistical inference. There are two main methods of statistical inference, confidence intervals, which are the subject of this chapter, and hypothesis testing, which is the subject of chapters 3, 4 and 5. Confidence intervals are used when we wish to estimate a population parameter and hypothesis testing is used when we wish to make a decision. The calculations involved in the two methods are often similar but the purpose is different.

If you have studied module S2 you will already have met confidence intervals.

2.2 Confidence interval for the mean of a normal distribution, standard deviation known

The method is best understood by considering a specific example.

The contents of a large batch of packets of baking powder are known to be normally distributed with standard deviation 7 g. The mean is unknown. A randomly selected packet is found to contain 193 g of baking powder. If this is the only information available the best estimate of the mean contents of the batch is 193 g. This is called a point estimate. However we know that if a different packet had been selected it would almost certainly have contained a different amount of baking powder. It is better to estimate the mean by an interval rather than by a single value. The interval expresses the fact that there is only a limited amount of information and so there is uncertainty in the estimate.

If an observation is taken from a standard normal distribution there is a probability of 0.95 that it will lie in the range ±1.96.

You may need to look back to SI, chapter 7 to revise the normal distribution.

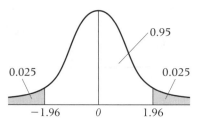

This means that there is a probability of 0.95 that an observation, x, from a normal distribution with mean μ and standard deviation σ will lie in the interval $\mu \pm 1.96\sigma$.

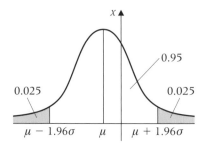

In the example of the packets of baking powder the value of x is known but the value of μ is unknown. If the interval is centred on x, i.e. $x \pm 1.96\sigma$, there is a probability of 0.95 that this interval will contain μ.

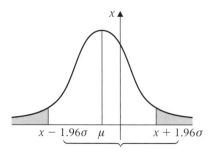

For the packets of baking powder the interval is

$$193 \pm 1.96 \times 7$$

i.e. 193 ± 13.7 or 179.3 to 206.7.

The interval is called a 95% confidence interval. This is because if intervals are calculated in this way then, in the long run, 95% of the intervals calculated will contain the population mean. This also means that 5% will not contain the population mean. Unfortunately there is no way of knowing, in a particular case, whether the interval calculated is one of the 95% which does contain μ or one of the 5% which does not contain μ. You can however say that it is much more likely to contain μ than not to contain μ.

The population mean, μ, is constant but unknown. The interval is known but will be different for each observation, x.

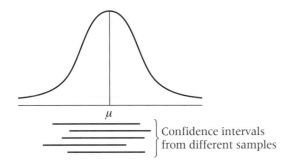

Confidence intervals from different samples

The level of confidence can be increased by widening the interval. For example a 99% confidence interval is

$$193 \pm 2.5758 \times 7$$

i.e. 193 ± 18.0 or 175.0 to 211.0.

It is not possible to calculate a 100% confidence interval.

> This is because there are no limits which contain 100% of a normal distribution.

Intuitively, it seems that a better estimate of μ, the mean contents of the packets of baking powder, will be obtained if we weigh the contents of more than one packet.

Four randomly selected packets were found to contain 193, 197, 212 and 184 g of baking powder. The sample mean is 196.5. The standard deviation of the mean of a sample of size four is $\dfrac{7}{\sqrt{4}} = 3.5$.

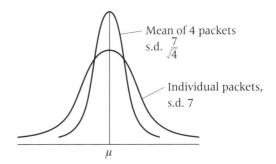

Mean of 4 packets s.d. $\dfrac{7}{\sqrt{4}}$

Individual packets, s.d. 7

A 95% confidence interval for the population mean is

$$196.5 \pm 1.96 \times 3.5$$

i.e. 196.5 ± 6.9 or 189.6 to 203.4.

Note 1. This interval is half the width of the 95% confidence interval calculated from the weight of a single packet. This has been achieved by increasing the sample size from one to four. However there is very little advantage in increasing a sample of size 21 to one of size 24. To halve the width of the interval you need to **multiply** the sample size by four.

Note 2. If the distribution is not normal the confidence interval will be inaccurate. This could be a major problem for the single observation but would be less serious for the sample of size four. For large samples the sample mean will be approximately normally distributed. Four is not a large sample but the mean of a sample of size four will come closer to following a normal distribution than will the distribution of a single observation.

> If $\bar{x}$ is the mean of a random sample of size n from a normal distribution with (unknown) mean μ and (known) standard deviation σ, a $100(1 - \alpha)\%$ confidence interval for μ is given by $\bar{x} \pm z_{\frac{\alpha}{2}} \dfrac{\sigma}{\sqrt{n}}$

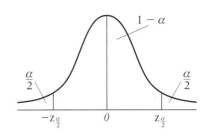

Worked example 2.1

A machine fills bottles with vinegar. The volumes of vinegar contained in these bottles are normally distributed with standard deviation 6 ml.

A random sample of five bottles from a large batch filled by the machine contained the following volumes, in millilitres, of vinegar:

986   996   984   990   1002

Calculate a 90% confidence interval for the mean volume of vinegar in bottles of this batch.

Solution

Sample mean = 991.6 ml
90% confidence interval for mean

$$991.6 \pm 1.6449 \times \frac{6}{\sqrt{5}}$$

i.e. 991.6 ± 4.41 or 987.2 to 996.0 ml

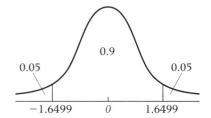

Answers are usually given to 3 sf. In this case, because the limits of the interval are close together 4 sf is reasonable.

Worked example 2.2

A food processor produces large batches of jars of jam. In each batch the weight of jam in a jar is known to be normally distributed with standard deviation 7 g. The weights, in grams, of the jam in a random sample of jars from a particular batch were:

481   455   468   457   469   463   469   458

(a) Calculate a 95% confidence interval for the mean weight of jam in this batch of jars.

(b) Assuming the mean weight is at the upper limit of the confidence interval calculated in **(a)**, calculate the limits within which 99% of weights of jam in these jars lies.

(c) The jars are claimed to contain 454 g of jam. Comment on this claim as it relates to this batch.

Solution

(a) Sample mean = 465.0
    95% confidence interval for mean weight of jam is

$$465 \pm 1.96 \times \frac{7}{\sqrt{8}}$$

i.e. 465 ± 4.851 or 460.1 to 469.9

Again 4 sf is reasonable.

(b) The upper limit of the confidence interval is 469.9.
    If the mean were 469.9, 99% of the weights of jam in the jars would lie in the range

$$469.9 \pm 2.5758 \times 7$$

i.e. 469.9 ± 18.0 or 451.9 to 487.9.

Here we are dealing with individual jars, not with sample means.

(c) 454 is below the lower limit of the confidence interval calculated in **(a)**. Hence it is safe to assume that the **mean** weight of jam in the jars exceeds 454 g.

However even if it is assumed that the mean is at the upper limit of the confidence interval, the interval calculated in **(b)** shows that some individual jars will contain less than 454 g.

EXERCISE 2A

1 The potency of a particular brand of aspirin tablets is known to be normally distributed with standard deviation 0.83. A random sample of tablets of this brand was tested and found to have potencies of

  58.7 58.4 59.3 60.4 59.8 59.4 57.7 60.3 61.0 58.2

Calculate:

(a) a 99% confidence interval for the mean potency of these tablets,

(b) a 95% confidence interval for the mean potency of these tablets,

(c) a 60% confidence interval for the mean potency of these tablets.

2 The diastolic blood pressures, in millimetres of mercury, of a population of healthy adults has standard deviation 12.8. The diastolic blood pressures of a random sample of members of an athletics club were measured with the following results:

  79.2 64.6 86.8 73.7 74.9 62.3

(a) Assuming the sample comes from a normal distribution with standard deviation 12.8 calculate:

  (i) a 90% confidence interval for the mean,

  (ii) a 95% confidence interval for the mean,

  (iii) a 99% confidence interval for the mean.

The diastolic blood pressures of a random sample of members of a chess club were also measured with the following results:

  84.6 93.2 104.6 106.7 76.3 78.2

(b) Assuming the sample comes from a normal distribution with standard deviation 12.8 calculate:

  (i) an 80% confidence interval for the mean,

  (ii) a 95% confidence interval for the mean,

  (iii) a 99% confidence interval for the mean.

(c) Comment on the diastolic blood pressure of members of each of the two clubs given that a population of healthy adults would have a mean of 84.8.

3 Applicants for an assembly job are to be given a test of manual dexterity. The times, in seconds, taken by a random sample of applicants to complete the test are

   63   229   165   77   49   74   67   59   66   102   81   72   59

Calculate a 90% confidence interval for the mean time taken by applicants. Assume the data comes from a normal distribution with standard deviation 57 s.

4 A rail traveller records the time she has to queue to buy a ticket. A random sample of times, in seconds, were

   136   120   67   255   84   99   280   55   78

(a) Assuming the data may be regarded as a random sample from a normal distribution with standard deviation 44 s, calculate a 95% confidence interval for the mean queuing time.

(b) Assume that the mean is at the lower limit of the confidence interval calculated in (a). Calculate limits within which 90% of her waiting times will lie.

(c) Comment on the station manager's claim that most passengers have to queue for less than 25 s to buy a ticket.

5 A food processor produces large batches of jars of pickles. In each batch, the gross weight of a jar is known to be normally distributed with standard deviation 7.5 g. (The gross weight is the weight of the jar plus the weight of the pickles.)
The gross weights, in grams, of a random sample from a particular batch were:

   514   485   501   486   502   496   509   491   497
   501   506   486   498   490   484   494   501   506
   490   487   507   496   505   498   499

(a) Calculate a 90% confidence interval for the mean gross weight of this batch.

The weight of an empty jar is known to be exactly 40 g.

(b) (i) What is the standard deviation of the weight of the pickles in a batch of jars?

   (ii) Assuming that the mean gross weight is at the upper limit of the confidence interval calculated in (a), calculate limits within which 99% of the weights of the pickles would lie.

(c) The jars are claimed to contain 454 g of pickles. Comment on this claim as it relates to this batch of jars.

2.3 Confidence interval for the mean based on a large sample

There are not many real life situations where we wish to use a confidence interval to estimate an unknown population mean when the population standard deviation is known. In most cases where the mean is unknown the standard deviation will also be unknown. If a large sample is available then this will provide a sufficiently good estimate of the standard deviation to enable a confidence interval for the mean to be calculated. The large sample also has the advantage of the sample mean being approximately normally distributed no matter what the distribution of the individual items.

>
> If a large random sample is available:
> **(a)** it can be used to provide a good estimate of the population standard deviation σ,
> **(b)** it is safe to assume that the mean is normally distributed.

2

This could occur in a mass production process where the mean length of components depends on the machine settings but the standard deviation is always the same. However it is unusual.

The definition of 'large' is arbitrary. A rule of thumb is that 'large' means at least 30.

Worked example 2.3

Seventy packs of butter, selected at random from a large batch delivered to a supermarket, are weighed. The mean weight is found to be 227 g and the standard deviation is found to be 7.5 g. Calculate a 95% confidence interval for the mean weight of all packs in the batch.

Solution

Seventy is a large sample and so although the standard deviation of the weights is not known we may use the standard deviation calculated from the sample. It does not matter whether the distribution is normal or not since the mean of a sample of 70 from any distribution may be modelled by a normal distribution.

95% confidence interval for the mean weight of packs of butter in the batch is

$$227 \pm 1.96 \times \frac{7.5}{\sqrt{70}}$$

i.e. 227 ± 1.76 or 225.2 to 228.8.

The sample is large and so it makes little difference whether the divisor n or $n - 1$ is used in calculating the standard deviation. Both will give very similar results. As the population standard deviation is being estimated from a sample it is correct to use the divisor $n - 1$.

At least 4 sf are required here. If the answer was rounded to 2 sf the interval would disappear completely.

Worked example 2.4

Shoe shop staff routinely measure the length of their customers' feet. Measurements of the length of one foot (without shoes) from each of 180 adult male customers yielded a mean length of 29.2 cm and a standard deviation of 1.47 cm.

(a) Calculate a 95% confidence interval for the mean length of male feet.

(b) Why was it not necessary to assume that the lengths of feet are normally distributed in order to calculate the confidence interval in **(a)**?

(c) What assumption was it necessary to make in order to calculate the confidence interval in **(a)**?

(d) Given that the lengths of male feet may be modelled by a normal distribution, and making any other necessary assumptions, calculate an interval within which 90% of the lengths of male feet will lie.

(e) In the light of your calculations in **(a)** and **(d)**, discuss briefly, the question 'Is a foot a foot long?' (One foot is 30.5 cm.)   [A]

Solution

(a) 95% confidence interval for mean length of male feet is

$$29.2 \pm 1.96 \times \frac{1.47}{\sqrt{180}}$$

i.e. 29.2 ± 0.215 or 28.99 to 29.41

(b) It is not necessary to assume lengths are normally distributed because the central limit theorem states that the mean of a large sample from any distribution will be approximately normally distributed.

See S1 section 7.11.

(c) To calculate the confidence interval in **(a)** we needed to assume that the sample could be treated as a random sample from the population of all male feet.

(d) 90% of male feet will lie in the interval

$$29.2 \pm 1.6449 \times 1.47$$

i.e. 29.2 ± 2.42 or 26.78 to 31.62

(e) The confidence interval calculated in **(a)** does not contain 30.5 and so it is very unlikely that the **mean** length of male feet is one foot. The interval calculated in **(d)** does contain 30.5 which indicates that some male feet are a foot long.

EXERCISE 2B

1 A telephone company selected a random sample of size 150 from those customers who had not paid their bills one month after they had been sent out. The mean amount owed by the customers in the sample was £97.50 and the standard deviation was £29.00.
Calculate a 90% confidence interval for the mean amount owed by all customers who had not paid their bills one month after they had been sent out.

2 A sample of 64 fish caught in the river Mirwell had a mean weight of 848 g with a standard deviation of 146 g. Assuming these may be regarded as a random sample of all the fish caught in the Mirwell, calculate, for the mean of this population:

   (a) a 95% confidence interval,

   (b) a 64% confidence interval.

3 A boat returns from a fishing trip holding 145 cod. The mean length of these cod is 74 cm and their standard deviation is 9 cm. The cod in the boat may be regarded as a random sample from a large shoal. The normal distribution may be regarded as an adequate model for the lengths of the cod in the shoal.

   (a) Calculate a 95% confidence interval for the mean length of cod in the shoal.

   (b) It is known that the normal distribution is not a good model for the weights of cod in a shoal. If the cod had been weighed, what difficulties, if any, would arise in calculating a confidence interval for the mean weight of cod in the shoal? Justify your answer.   [A]

4 A sweet shop sells chocolates which appear, at first sight, to be identical. Of a random sample of 80 chocolates, 61 had hard centres and the rest soft centres. The chocolates are in the shape of circular discs and the diameters, in centimetres, of the 19 soft-centred chocolates were:

   2.79 2.63 2.84 2.77 2.81 2.69 2.66 2.71 2.62 2.75
   2.77 2.72 2.81 2.74 2.79 2.77 2.67 2.69 2.75

The mean diameter of the 61 hard-centred chocolates was 2.690 cm.

   (a) If the diameters of both hard-centred and soft-centred chocolates are known to be normally distributed with standard deviation 0.042 cm, calculate a 95% confidence interval for the mean diameter of,

   (i) the soft-centred chocolates,

   (ii) the hard-centred chocolates.

   (b) Calculate an interval within which approximately 95% of the diameters of hard-centred chocolates will lie.

   (c) Discuss, briefly, how useful knowledge of the diameter of a chocolate is in determining whether it is hard- or soft-centred.   [A]

5 Packets of baking powder have a nominal weight of 200 g. The
distribution of weights is normal and the standard deviation is
10 g. Average quantity system legislation states that, if the
nominal weight is 200 g,

- the average weight must be at least 200 g,
- not more than 2.5% of packages may weigh less than 191 g,
- not more than 1 in 1000 packages may weigh less than
  182 g.

A random sample of 30 packages had the following weights:

218 207 214 189 211 206 203 217 183 186
219 213 207 214 203 204 195 197 213 212
188 221 217 184 186 216 198 211 216 200

(a) Calculate a 95% confidence interval for the mean weight.

(b) Assuming that the mean is at the lower limit of the
interval calculated in **(a)**, what proportion of packets
would weigh,

(i) less than 191 g,

(ii) less than 182 g?

(c) Discuss the suitability of the packets from the point of
view of the average quantity system. A simple
adjustment will change the mean weight of future
packages. Changing the standard deviation is possible
but very expensive. Without carrying out any further
calculations, discuss any adjustments you might
recommend.   [A]

Worked example 2.5

Solid fuel is packed in sacks which are then weighed on scales. It
is known that if the full sack weighs μ kg the weight recorded by
the scales will be normally distributed with mean μ kg and
standard deviation 0.36 kg.

A particular full sack was weighed four times and the weights
recorded were 34.7, 34.4, 35.1 and 34.6 kg.

(a) Calculate a 95% confidence interval for the weight of this
full sack.

(b) State the width of the interval calculated in **(a)**.

(c) What percentage would be associated with a confidence
interval of width 0.3 kg?

(d) How many times would this full sack have to be weighed so
that a 95% confidence interval for the weight would be of
width 0.3 kg?

Solution

(a) $\bar{x} = 34.7$

95% confidence interval for the mean is

$$34.7 \pm 1.96 \times \frac{0.36}{\sqrt{4}}$$

i.e. 34.7 ± 0.353 or 34.35 to 35.05

(b) width of interval is $2 \times 0.353 = 0.706$

(c) $0.3 = 2z \times \dfrac{0.36}{\sqrt{4}}$

$z = 0.833$

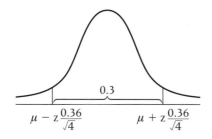

% confidence $= 100\{0.7977 - (1 - 0.7977)\}$
i.e. 59.54 or approximately 60%.

A 60% confidence interval would have width approximately 0.3 kg.

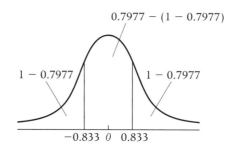

(d) $0.3 = 2 \times 1.96 \times \dfrac{0.36}{\sqrt{n}}$

$\sqrt{n} = 4.704 \qquad n = 22.1.$

If the sack was weighed 22 times a 95% confidence interval would be of width approximately 0.3 kg.

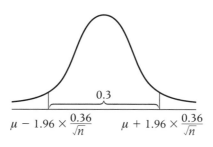

Worked example 2.6

Electricians working on a building site use lighting cable supplied in 100 m coils. The last remaining piece of cable on each coil is often wasted because it is too short. It is believed that the length, X cm, of wasted pieces of cable may be modelled by a random variable which follows a rectangular distribution with probability density function

$$f(x) = \begin{cases} \dfrac{1}{k} & 0 \leq x \leq k \\ 0 & \text{otherwise} \end{cases}$$

This distribution has mean k/2 and variance $k^2/12$.

(a) A random sample of 120 wasted pieces of cable was measured. The sample mean length was found to be 210 cm. Use this value to estimate k.

(b) Use your estimate of k to estimate the standard deviation of the distribution.

(c) Find an approximate 95% confidence interval for the mean of X.

(d) Give two reasons why this confidence interval is approximate rather than exact.

The longest piece of wasted cable was 510 cm in length.

(e) Explain why this makes it unlikely that the rectangular distribution provides an adequate model for the length of wasted pieces of cable. [A]

Solution

(a) $\dfrac{\hat{k}}{2} = 210$ $\quad \hat{k} = 420$

$\hat{k}$ is our estimate of k.

(b) Estimated variance $= \dfrac{420^2}{12} = 14\,700$

estimated standard deviation $= 121.24$

(c) The confidence interval is based on a large sample and so you can use the normal distribution.
Approximate 95% confidence interval is

$$210 \pm 1.96 \times \frac{121.24}{\sqrt{120}}$$

i.e. 210 ± 21.7 or 188.3 to 231.7

(d) The sample mean will not follow a normal distribution exactly. The standard deviation used is only an estimate.

(e) Upper limit of confidence interval for mean is 231.7 giving an upper limit for k of $2 \times 231.7 = 463.4$. For a rectangular distribution $0 < x < k$. An observation of 510 is not consistent with this – rectangular model inadequate.

Worked example 2.7 _____

(a) A sample of adult female bears observed in the wild had the following weights in kilograms.

98 57 71 107 109

The data may be regarded as a random sample from a normally distributed population with a standard deviation of 11 kg.
Calculate a 99% confidence interval for the mean weight of adult female bears.

(b) A sample of adult male bears is also weighed and used to calculate both a 90% and a 95% confidence interval for μ, the mean weight of the population of adult male bears, (i.e. both confidence intervals are calculated from the same sample).

Find the probability that:

(i) the 90% confidence interval does not contain μ,

(ii) the 90% confidence interval does not contain μ but the 95% confidence interval does contain μ,

(iii) the 95% confidence interval contains μ, given that the 90% confidence interval does not contain μ,

(iv) the 90% confidence interval contains μ, given that the 95% confidence interval does not contain μ.

(c) Find the probability that the confidence interval calculated in **(a)** does not contain the mean weight of adult female bears and the 90% confidence interval in **(b)** does not contain μ.   [A]

Solution

(a) $\bar{x} = 88.4$

99% confidence interval for the mean is

$$88.4 \pm 2.5758 \times \frac{11}{\sqrt{5}}$$

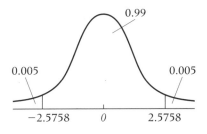

i.e 88.4 ± 12.7 or 75.7 to 101.1

(i) There is a probability of 0.9 that a 90% confidence interval contains μ and so there is a probability of $1 - 0.9 = 0.1$ that a 90% confidence interval does not contain μ.

(ii) If the 95% confidence interval contains μ but the 90% confidence interval does not contain μ then $\bar{x}$ must lie in the shaded area.

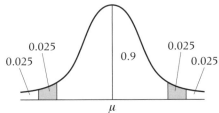

Probability is 0.05.

(iii) P(95% contains μ | 90% does not contain μ)

$$= \frac{\text{P(95\% contains } \mu \text{ and 90\% does not contain } \mu)}{\text{P(90\% does not contain } \mu)}$$

$$= \frac{0.05}{0.1} = 0.5.$$

(iv) If the 95% confidence interval does not contain μ it is impossible for the 90% confidence interval to contain μ.

The probability is 0.

(c) The probability that the 99% confidence interval calculated in **(a)** does not contain the mean weight of female bears is $1 - 0.99 = 0.01$.

The probability the 90% confidence interval calculated in **(b)** does not contain μ is $1 - 0.9 = 0.1$.

Assuming that these two samples are independent the required probability is $0.01 \times 0.1 = 0.001$.

EXERCISE 2C

1 A random sample of experimental components for use in aircraft engines was tested to destruction under extreme conditions. The survival times, X days, of ten components were as follows:

      207   381   111   673   234   294   897   144   418   554

  (a) Assuming that the survival time, under these conditions, for all the experimental components is normally distributed with standard deviation 240 days, calculate a 90% confidence interval for the mean of X.

  (b) State the probability that the confidence interval calculated in **(a)** does not contain the mean of X.

2 A car manufacturer purchases large quantities of a particular component. The working lives of the components are known to be normally distributed with mean 2400 hours and standard deviation 650 hours. The manufacturer is concerned about the large variability and the supplier undertakes to improve the design so that the standard deviation is reduced to 300 hours.

A random sample of five of the new components is tested and found to last

      2730   3120   2980   2680   2800 hours.

Assuming that the lives of the new components are normally distributed with standard deviation 300 hours:

  (a) (i) Calculate a 90% confidence interval for their mean working life.

      (ii) How many of the new components would it be necessary to test in order to make the width of a 95% confidence interval for the mean just less than 100 hours?

  (b) Lives of components commonly follow a distribution which is not normal. If the assumption of normality is invalid, comment briefly on the amount of uncertainty in your answers to **(a)(i)** and **(ii)**.

  (c) Is there any reason to doubt the assumption that the standard deviation of the lives of the new components is 300 hours?   [A]

3 A machine produces plastic balls for use in an industrial process. It incorporates a device which automatically recycles those balls whose weights are outside certain limits. The weights of the balls produced (measured as a deviation, in grams, from the minimum value) may be regarded as a random variable, X, with probability density function

$$f(x) = \begin{cases} k(2-x) & 0 \leqslant x \leqslant 2 \\ 0 & \text{otherwise} \end{cases}$$

(a) Show that k = 0.5.

(b) Find the mean and the standard deviation of X correct to 3 significant figures.

(c) The mean of the distribution may change from day to day but the shape and standard deviation do not. A random sample of size 40 yields a sample mean of 0.90. Calculate an approximate 90% confidence interval for the population mean. Explain the relevance of the central limit theorem to your calculations. [A]

4 A supermarket sells cartons of tea bags. The weight, in grams, of the contents of the cartons in any batch is known to be normally distributed with mean μ_T and standard deviation 4. In order to compare the actual contents with that claimed by the supplier, a manager weighed the contents of a random sample of five cartons from a large batch and obtained the following results, in grams:

196   202   198   197   190

(a) Calculate:

(i) a 95% confidence interval for μ_T,

(ii) a 60% confidence interval for μ_T.

The manager intends to do the same thing tomorrow (i.e. to weigh the contents of a random sample of cartons of tea and to use the data collected to calculate both a 95% and a 60% confidence interval).

(b) State the probability that:

(i) the 95% confidence interval she calculates will not contain μ_T,

(ii) neither of the confidence intervals she calculates will contain μ_T.

The manager also intends to weigh the contents of jars of coffee from a batch in order to calculate a 95% and a 60% confidence interval for the mean contents, μ_C, of jars in the batch. However, in this case, the 95% confidence interval will be calculated from one random sample and the 60% confidence interval calculated from a second, independent, random sample.

(c) Find the probability that neither the 60% nor the 95% confidence interval for the mean contents of jars of coffee will contain μ_C. [A]

5 Batteries supplied to a large institution for use in electric clocks had a mean working life of 960 days with a standard deviation of 135 days.

A sample from a new supplier had working lives of

1020, 998, 894, 921, 843, 1280, 1302, 782, 694, 1350 days.

Assume that the data may be regarded as a random sample from a normal distribution with standard deviation 135 days.

(a) For the working lives of batteries from the new supplier, calculate a 95% confidence interval for the mean.

(b) The institution would like batteries with a large mean. Compare the two sources of supply.

(c) State the width of the confidence interval calculated in (a).

(d) What percentage would be associated with an interval of width 100 days calculated from the data above?

(e) How large a sample would be needed to calculate a 90% confidence interval of width approximately 100 days? [A]

6 In an attempt to economise on her telephone bill, Debbie times her calls and ensures that they never last longer than four minutes.

The length of the calls, T, minutes, may be regarded as a random variable with probability density function

See page 19, question 3.

$$f(t) = \begin{cases} kt & 0 \leqslant t \leqslant 4 \\ 0 & \text{otherwise} \end{cases} \quad \text{where k is a constant}$$

(a) (i) Show that k = 0.125.

(ii) Find the mean and standard deviation of T.

(b) Debbie's next telephone bill showed that 120 calls had a mean length of 3.8 minutes. Assuming that the standard deviation of the length of calls was as calculated in (a), calculate a 90% confidence interval for the mean length of Debbie's calls.

(c) What assumption have you had to make in order to calculate the confidence interval in (b)?

(d) Comment on whether the probability distribution defined above provides an adequate model for the length of Debbie's calls. [A]

2.4 Confidence interval for the mean of a normal distribution, standard deviation unknown

A 95% confidence interval for the mean of a normal distribution is given by

$$\bar{x} \pm 1.96\frac{\sigma}{\sqrt{n}}$$

If σ is unknown it can be estimated from the sample (provided the sample is of size two or greater). However unless n is large there will be a considerable amount of uncertainty in this estimate, s. This uncertainty can be allowed for by multiplying $\frac{s}{\sqrt{n}}$ by a number larger than 1.96. The size of the number required has been calculated and tabulated in the **t distribution**. The required value of t will depend on the amount of uncertainty. The larger the sample, the less the uncertainty. The amount of uncertainty is measured by the **degrees of freedom**. For this unit all you need to know is that an estimate of σ from a sample of size n has $n-1$ degrees of freedom.

> This is often referred to as Student's t distribution. This is tabulated in Table 5 in the Appendix.

> The number of degrees of freedom is usually denoted ν.

> An estimate of a population standard deviation calculated from a random sample of size n has $n-1$ degrees of freedom. -

In section 2.3 a sample of four packets of baking powder weighed

193 197 212 and 184 g.

If the standard deviation is unknown we can use a calculator to find s = 11.676, $\bar{x}$ = 196.5

The sample is of size four and so there are three degrees of freedom. For a 95% confidence interval the appropriate value of t is 3.182.

> P = 0.975, ν = 3

Table 5 Percentage points of the student's t distribution

The table gives the values of x satisfying $P(X \leqslant x) = p$, where X is a random variable having the Student's t distribution with ν-degrees of freedom.

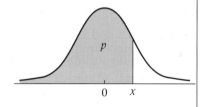

ν \ p	0.9	0.95	0.975	0.99	0.995
1	3.078	6.314	12.706	31.821	63.657
2	1.886	2.920	4.303	6.965	9.925
3	1.638	2.353	3.182	4.541	5.841
4	1.533	2.132	2.776	3.747	4.604
5	1.476	2.015	2.571	3.365	4.032

ν \ p	0.9	0.95	0.975	0.99	0.995
29	1.311	1.699	2.045	2.462	2.756
30	1.310	1.697	2.042	2.457	2.750
31	1.309	1.696	2.040	2.453	2.744
32	1.309	1.694	2.037	2.449	2.738
33	1.308	1.692	2.035	2.445	2.733

A 95% confidence interval for the mean is given by

$$196.5 \pm 3.182 \times \frac{11.676}{\sqrt{4}}$$

i.e. 196.5 ± 18.6 or 177.9 to 215.1

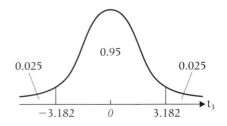

> If $\bar{x}$ is the mean of a random sample of size n from a normal distribution with mean μ, a $100(1 - \alpha)$% confidence interval for μ is given by
>
> $$\bar{x} \pm t_{\frac{\alpha}{2}, n-1} \frac{s}{\sqrt{n}}$$

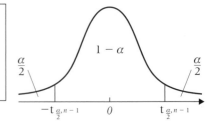

Worked example 2.8

A random sample of patients who had been treated by the casualty department of a large hospital were asked to state how long they had waited before seeing a doctor. The replies, in minutes, were as follows:

    12   109   35   63   54   72   10

(a) Assuming a normal distribution calculate a 90% confidence interval for the mean stated waiting time.

(b) Comment on the hospital administrator's claim that the mean waiting time in casualty before seeing a doctor is 15 minutes.

Solution

(a) $\bar{x} = 50.71$ $s = 35.16$
    sample size $= 7$ degrees of freedom $= 6$

    90% confidence interval for the mean

$$50.71 \pm 1.943 \times \frac{35.16}{\sqrt{7}}$$

    i.e. 50.7 ± 25.8 or 24.9 to 76.5 minutes.

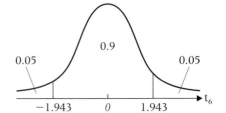

(b) As 15 lies below the confidence interval it appears that the hospital administrator underestimates the average waiting time in casualty. (However as the calculation is based on patients' recollections rather than accurate timings the data may be unreliable.)

Worked example 2.9

A machine produces plastic boxes for compact discs. The widths of the discs follow a normal distribution and the standard deviation is believed to be 0.04 mm.

A random sample of six boxes from a particular day's production is measured and found to have widths, in mm, of

118.24   118.27   118.35   118.21   118.29   118.26

(a) Calculate a 95% confidence interval for the mean width of boxes produced that day:

   (i) assuming the standard deviation is 0.04 mm,

   (ii) making no assumption about the standard deviation.

(b) Give one argument in favour of using the confidence interval calculated in **(a)(i)** and one argument in favour of using the confidence interval calculated in **(a)(ii)**.

Solution

(a) **(i)** $\bar{x} = 118.270$

95% confidence interval for mean width of boxes is

$$118.270 \pm 1.96 \times \frac{0.04}{\sqrt{6}}$$

i.e. 118.270 ± 0.032 or 118.238 to 118.302

  (ii) $s = 0.0477$

95% confidence interval for mean width of boxes is

$$118.270 \pm 2.571 \times \frac{0.0477}{\sqrt{6}}$$

i.e. 118.270 ± 0.050 or 118.220 to 118.320

(b) The confidence interval calculated in **(a)(i)** uses an estimate of standard deviation based on past experience. This is likely to be more accurate than an estimate made from the current small sample. The fact that the current sample yields an estimate of standard deviation close to 0.04 means there is no reason to suppose that the standard deviation has changed.

The confidence interval calculated in **(a)(ii)** makes no assumption about the standard deviation being unchanged and is valid whether or not this is the case.

EXERCISE 2D

1 Before its annual overhaul, the mean operating time of an automatic machine was 103 s. After the annual overhaul, the following random sample of operating times (in seconds) was obtained:

90   97   101   92   101   95   95   98   96   95

(a) Assuming that the time taken by the machine to perform the operation is normally distributed find 95% confidence limits for the mean operating time after the overhaul.

(b) Comment on the effectiveness of the overhaul.

2 A random sample of 12 unsalted packs of butter from a large batch had the following weights:

219 226 217 224 223 216 221 228 215 229 225 229

Find, for the mean weight of the unsalted packs of butter in the batch:

(a) an 80% confidence interval,
(b) a 90% confidence interval,
(c) a 95% confidence interval,
(d) a 99% confidence interval.

3 The resistances (in ohms) of a sample from a batch of resistors were

2314 2456 2389 2361 2360 2332 2402

Past experience suggests that the standard deviation, σ, is 35 Ω.

(a) Calculate a 95% confidence interval for the mean resistance of the batch:
  (i) assuming $\sigma = 35$,
  (ii) making no assumption about the standard deviation.
(b) Compare the merits of the confidence intervals calculated in **(a)**. [A]

4 An automatic dispensing machine may be set to dispense predetermined quantities of liquid into bottles. Past experience suggests that the standard deviation of the amount dispensed is 2.6 ml.

An operator selected six recently filled bottles at random and measured the amounts of liquid which had been dispensed. The amounts, in ml, were

512 510 508 515 511 517

(a) Assuming that the sample comes from a normal distribution, calculate a 95% confidence interval for the mean if:
  (i) the standard deviation is 2.6 ml,
  (ii) no assumption is made about the standard deviation.
(b) Comment on the relative suitability in these circumstances of the two confidence intervals you have calculated. [A]

5 Stud anchors are used in the construction industry. Samples are tested by embedding them in concrete and applying a steadily increasing load until the anchor fails. A sample of six tests gave the following maximum loads in kN:

27.0 30.5 28.0 23.0 27.5 26.5

(a) Assuming a normal distribution for the maximum load calculate a 95% confidence interval for the mean.
(b) If the mean was at the lower end of the interval calculated in **(a)** estimate the value, k, which the maximum load would exceed with probability 0.99. Assume the standard deviation estimated is an accurate assessment of the population standard deviation.

Safety regulations require that the greatest load which may be applied under working conditions is $\dfrac{(\bar{x} - 2s)}{3}$ where $\bar{x}$ and s are calculated from a sample of six tests.

(c) Calculate this value and comment on the adequacy of this regulation in these circumstances. [A]

6 A car manufacturer introduces a new method of assembling a particular component. A sample of assembly times (minutes) taken after the new method had become established was:

   27 19 68 41 17 52 35 72 38

(a) Calculate a 99% confidence interval for the mean assembly time.

(b) State any assumptions it was necessary to make in order to calculate the confidence interval in **(a)**.

A larger random sample of 45 assembly times had a mean of 36.3 minutes with a standard deviation of 9.8 minutes.

(c) Calculate a 99% confidence for the mean assembly time.

(d) Was it necessary to make the assumptions of **(b)** in order to calculate the interval in **(c)**? Explain your answer. [A]

Key point summary

I If $\bar{x}$ is the mean of a random sample of size n from a   *p25*
normal distribution with (unknown) mean μ and
(known) standard deviation σ, a $100(1 - \alpha)\%$
confidence interval for μ is given by $\bar{x} \pm z_{\frac{\alpha}{2}} \dfrac{\sigma}{\sqrt{n}}$.

2 If a large random sample is available: *p29*

   (a) it can be used to provide a good estimate of the population standard deviation σ,

   (b) it is safe to assume that the mean is normally distributed.

3 An estimate of a population standard deviation   *p39*
calculated from a random sample of size n has
$n - 1$ degrees of freedom.

4 If $\bar{x}$ is the mean of a random sample of size n from   *p40*
a normal distribution with mean μ, a $100(1 - \alpha)\%$
confidence interval for μ is given by

   $$\bar{x} \pm t_{\frac{\alpha}{2}, n-1} \dfrac{s}{\sqrt{n}}$$

Test yourself	What to review
1 The lengths of components produced by a machine are normally distributed with standard deviation 0.005 cm. A random sample of components measured 1.002 1.007 1.016 1.009 1.003 cm. Calculate a 95% confidence interval for the population mean.	*Section 2.2*
2 State the probability that an 85% confidence interval for μ does not contain μ.	*Section 2.2*
3 A population standard deviation is estimated from a random sample of size 12. How many degrees of freedom are associated with this estimate?	*Section 2.4*
4 The weights, in grams, of a random sample of free-range eggs sold by a health food cooperative were 47 49 56 53 55 46 59 Assuming the weights follow a normal distribution, calculate a 90% confidence interval for its mean.	*Section 2.4*
5 Comment on the claim that the mean weight of the eggs in question 4 is 55.5 g.	*Section 2.4*
6 The contents of a random sample of 80 tins of vindaloo cooking sauce from a large batch were weighed. The sample mean content was 284.2 g and the standard deviation, s, was found to be 4.1 g. Calculate a 95% confidence interval for the population mean.	*Section 2.3*
7 How would your answer to question 6 be affected if it was later discovered that the batch contained tins which had been produced on two different machines and the distribution of the weights was bimodal?	*Section 2.3*
8 How would your answer to question 6 be affected if it was later discovered that the sample was not random?	*Section 2.3*

Test yourself ANSWERS

8 If the sample was not random this would make the confidence interval unreliable. For example, the sample of tins could all have come from the same machine leading to a biased result.

7 It would not affect the answer. The sample is stated to be a random sample from the whole batch and the central limit theorem applies to all distributions whether bimodal or not.

6 283.30–285.10.

5 Although 55.5 is higher than the sample mean it lies within the confidence interval. There is therefore no convincing evidence that the mean is not 55.5 g as claimed.

1 1.0030–1.0118.   **2** 0.15.   **3** 11.   **4** 48.5–55.8.

CHAPTER 3
Hypothesis testing

Learning objectives

After studying this chapter you should be able to:

- define a null and alternative hypothesis
- define the significance level of a hypothesis test
- identify a critical region
- understand whether to use a one- or a two-tailed test
- understand what is meant by a **Type 1** and **Type 2** error
- test a hypothesis about a population mean based on a sample from a normal distribution with known standard deviation.

> If you have studied module S3 you will have already met these terms.

> This hypothesis test is not in S3. The population mean is denoted by μ.

3.1 Forming a hypothesis

One of the most important applications of statistics is to use a *sample* to test an idea, or *hypothesis*, you have regarding a population. This is one of the methods of statistical inference referred to in section 2.1.

Conclusions can never be absolutely certain but the risk of your conclusion being incorrect can be quantified (measured) and can enable you to identify *statistically significant* results.

> Statistically significant results require overwhelming evidence.

In any experiment, you will have your own idea or hypothesis as to how you expect the results to turn out.

A **Null Hypothesis,** written H_0, is set up at the start of any hypothesis test. This null hypothesis is a statement which defines the population and so always contains '=' signs, never '>', '<' or '≠'.

An example of a Null Hypothesis which you will meet in Worked example 3.1 of this chapter is:

H_0 Population mean lifetime of bulbs, $\mu = 500$ hours.

Usually, you are hoping to show that the Null Hypothesis is **not** true and so the **Alternative Hypothesis**, written H_1, is often the hypothesis you want to establish. Worked example 3.1 has:

H_1 Population mean lifetime of bulbs, $\mu > 500$ hours.

> The **null hypothesis** is only abandoned in the face of overwhelming evidence that it cannot explain the experimental results.
> Rather like in a court of law where the defendant is considered innocent until the evidence proves without doubt that he or she is guilty, the H_0 is accepted as true until test results show overwhelmingly that they cannot be explained if it was true.

> It often seems strange to students that they may want to show that H_0 is **not** true but, considering the examples of H_0 and H_1 given here, a manufacturer may well hope to show that bulbs have a **longer** than average lifetime.

> A hypothesis test needs two hypotheses identified at the beginning: H_0 the **Null Hypothesis** and H_1 the **Alternative Hypothesis**.

> H_0 states that a situation is unchanged, that a population parameter takes its usual value
> H_1 states that the parameter has increased, decreased or just changed

3.2 One- and two-tailed tests

Tests which involve an H_1 with a $>$ or $<$ sign are called **one-tailed** tests because we are expecting to find just an increase or just a decrease.

Tests which involve an H_1 with a $\neq$ sign are called **two-tailed** tests as they consider any change (whether it be an increase or decrease).

For example, if data were collected on the amount of weekly pocket money given to a random selection of children aged between 12 and 14 in a rural area, and also in a city, it may be that you are interested in investigating whether children in the city are given **more** pocket money than children in rural areas. Therefore, you may set up your hypotheses as:

H_0 Average pocket money of children is the same in the rural area and in the city, or

$$\mu \text{ (city)} = \mu \text{ (rural)}$$

H_1 Average pocket money **greater** in city, or

$$\mu \text{ (city)} > \mu \text{ (rural)}$$

This is an example of a **one-tailed** test.

> **One-tailed** tests will generally involve words such as:
> better or worse,
> faster or slower,
> more or less,
> bigger or smaller,
> increase or decrease.
> In Worked example 3.1,
> H_1 $\mu > 500$ hours indicates a **one-tailed** test.

However, if you were monitoring the weight of items produced in a factory, it would be likely that **any** change, be it an increase or decrease, would be a problem and there would not necessarily be any reason to expect a change of a specific type.
In this case, typical hypotheses would be:

H_0 Population mean weight is 35 g

$$\mu = 35\text{g}$$

H_1 Population mean weight **is not** 35 g

$$\mu \neq 35\text{g}$$

This is an example of a **two-tailed** test.

> **Two-tailed** tests will generally involve words such as:
> different or difference,
> change,
> affected.

A **two-tailed** test is one where H_1 involves testing for any (non-directional) change in a parameter.

A **one-tailed** test is one where H_1 involves testing specifically for an increase or for a decrease (change in one direction only).

3.3 Testing a hypothesis about a population mean

3

Carrying out a hypothesis test to determine whether a population mean is significantly different from the suggested value stated in H_0 involves calculating a **test statistic** from a sample taken from the population.

It is very important that it can be assumed or known that the sample has been selected **randomly.** If the sample were not selected randomly, then valid conclusions regarding the whole population cannot be made since the sample may only represent one part of that population.

As the test involves the population mean, it is the **sample mean**, $\bar{x}$, which must be evaluated. Since this test concerns a sample taken from a *normal* distribution, we also know that the sample means follow a normal distribution with mean equal to μ and with standard deviation equal to $\frac{\sigma}{\sqrt{n}}$.

See book S1 chapter 7.

The **test statistic** simply standardises the sample mean, $\bar{x}$, so that the result can be compared to critical z values.

Test statistic $= \dfrac{\bar{x} - \mu}{\dfrac{\sigma}{\sqrt{n}}}$

3.4 Critical region and significance level of test

The **critical region** is the range of values of the test statistic which is so unlikely to occur when H_0 is true, that it will lead to the conclusion that H_0 is not true. The **significance level** of a test determines what is considered the level of overwhelming evidence necessary for the decision to conclude that H_0 is not true. It is the probability of wrongly rejecting a true H_0. The smaller the significance level, the more overwhelming the evidence required. Common values used for **significance levels** are 1%, 5% or 10%.

The test introduced in this chapter is based on a sample from a normal distribution. Therefore, the **critical region** is identified by finding critical z values from Table 4, 'Percentage

Table 4 in the AQA Formulae book.

points of the normal distribution', in exactly the same way as the z values were found in order for confidence intervals to be constructed.

See chapter 2.

Some examples of critical regions are illustrated below.

One-tailed tests at 5% significance level

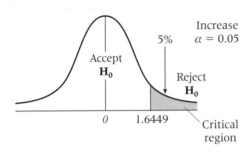

A 5% significance level is denoted $\alpha = 0.05$.

$z_\alpha = 1.6449$.

$z_\alpha = -1.6449$.

One-tailed tests at 1% significance level

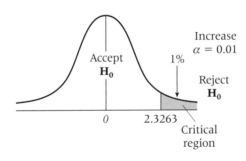

A 1% significance level is denoted $\alpha = 0.01$.

$z_\alpha = 2.3263$.

$z_\alpha = -2.3263$.

Two-tailed tests at 5% and 10% significance levels

Two critical values – change at both ends is considered.

> A 10% significance level is denoted $\alpha = 0.10$.

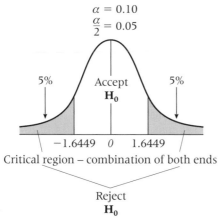

$\alpha = 0.10$
$\frac{\alpha}{2} = 0.05$

5%   Accept $\mathbf{H_0}$ 5%

$-1.6449 \quad 0 \quad 1.6449$

Critical region – combination of both ends

Reject $\mathbf{H_0}$

> $z_{\frac{\alpha}{2}} = \pm 1.6449 \quad \alpha = 0.10.$

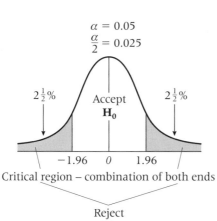

$\alpha = 0.05$
$\frac{\alpha}{2} = 0.025$

$2\frac{1}{2}\%$ Accept $\mathbf{H_0}$ $2\frac{1}{2}\%$

$-1.96 \quad 0 \quad 1.96$

Critical region – combination of both ends

Reject $\mathbf{H_0}$

> $z_{\frac{\alpha}{2}} = \pm 1.96 \quad \alpha = 0.05.$

The **critical region** or **critical value** identifies the range of extreme values which lead to the **rejection** of $\mathbf{H_0}$.

The **significance level**, α, of a test is the probability that a test statistic lies in the extreme critical region, if $\mathbf{H_0}$ is true. It determines the level of overwhelming evidence deemed necessary for the rejection of $\mathbf{H_0}$.

3.5 General procedure for carrying out a hypothesis test

The general procedure for hypothesis testing is:
1 Write down $\mathbf{H_0}$ and $\mathbf{H_1}$ 4 Identify the critical region
2 Decide which test to use   5 Calculate the test statistic
3 Decide on the significance level   6 Make your conclusion

Worked example 3.1

The lifetimes (hours) of Xtralong light bulbs are known to be normally distributed with a standard deviation of 90 hours.

A random sample of ten light bulbs is taken from a large batch produced in the Xtralong factory after an expensive machinery overhaul.

The lifetimes of these bulbs were measured as

523   556   678   429   558   498   399   515   555   699 hours.

Before the overhaul the mean life was 500 hours.

Investigate, at the 5% significance level, whether the mean life of Xtralong light bulbs has increased after the overhaul.

> The bulbs may appear to have a longer mean lifetime now but this may not be statistically significant.

Solution

The important facts to note are:

We are testing whether the mean is still 500 hours or whether an increase has occurred.

This means that $\mathbf{H_0}$ is $\mu = 500$ hours
and $\mathbf{H_1}$ is $\mu > 500$ hours a **one-tailed** test.

The test is at the **5%** significance level.

The lifetimes are normally distributed with known standard deviation of 90 hours.

The hypothesis test is carried out as follows:

$\mathbf{H_0}$ $\mu = 500$ hours
$\mathbf{H_1}$ $\mu > 500$ hours $\alpha = 0.05$

From tables, the critical value is $z = 1.6449$ for this one-tailed test.

The sample mean, $\bar{x} = 541$ hours, from a sample with $n = 10$.

The population standard deviation is known, $\sigma = 90$ hours.

Therefore the test statistic

$$\frac{\bar{x} - \mu}{\frac{\sigma}{\sqrt{n}}} = \frac{541 - 500}{\frac{90}{\sqrt{10}}} = 1.44$$

Conclusion

$1.44 < 1.6449$ for this one-tailed test, hence $\mathbf{H_0}$ is accepted.

There is no significant evidence to suggest that an increase in mean lifetime has occurred since the overhaul.

> Notice that we have not **proved** that $\mu = 500$ hours but we have shown that if $\mu = 500$ hours, a sample mean of 541 is not a particularly unlikely event.

Worked example 3.2

A forestry worker decided to keep records of the first year's growth of pine seedlings. Over several years, she found that the growth followed a normal distribution with a mean of 11.5 cm and a standard deviation of 2.5 cm.

Last year, she used an experimental soil preparation for the pine seedlings and the first year's growth of a sample of eight of the seedlings was

    7   22   19   15   11   18   17   15 cm.

Investigate, at the 1% significance level, whether there has been a change in the mean growth. Assume the standard deviation has not changed.

Solution

The important facts to note are:

We are testing whether the mean is 11.5 cm or not.

This means that H_0 is $\mu = 11.5$ cm
          and H_1 is $\mu \neq 11.5$ cm a **two-tailed** test.

The test is at the **1%** significance level.

The growth is normally distributed with known standard deviation of 2.5 cm.

The hypothesis test is carried out as follows:

  H_0 $\mu = 11.5$ cm
  H_1 $\mu \neq 11.5$ cm $\alpha = 0.01$

From tables, the critical values are $z_{\frac{\alpha}{2}} = \pm 2.5758$ for this two-tailed test.

The sample mean, $\bar{x} = 15.5$, from a sample with n = 8.

The population standard deviation is known, $\sigma = 2.5$ cm.

Therefore the test statistic
$$\frac{\bar{x} - \mu}{\frac{\sigma}{\sqrt{n}}} = \frac{15.5 - 11.5}{\frac{2.5}{\sqrt{8}}} = 4.53$$

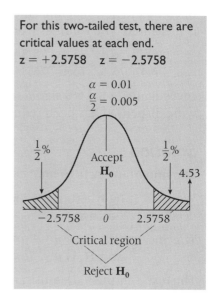

For this two-tailed test, there are critical values at each end.
z = +2.5758   z = −2.5758

$\alpha = 0.01$
$\frac{\alpha}{2} = 0.005$

$\frac{1}{2}$% Accept H_0 $\frac{1}{2}$%   4.53

−2.5758   0   2.5758

Critical region

Reject H_0

Conclusion

4.53 > 2.5758 for this two-tailed test, hence H_0 is clearly rejected.

There is significant evidence to suggest that a change in mean growth has occurred.

It is clear from the data that the mean has **increased**. You can conclude that the mean has **changed** or that it has **increased**. Either would be accepted in an examination.

Worked example 3.3

The owner of a small vineyard has an old bottling machine which is used for filling bottles with his wine. The bottles contain a nominal 75 cl of wine.

The old machine is known to dispense volumes of wine which are normally distributed with mean 76.4 cl and a standard deviation of 0.9 cl.

The owner is concerned that his old machine is becoming unreliable and he decides to purchase a new bottling machine. The manufacturer assures the owner that the new machine will dispense volumes which are normally distributed with a standard deviation of 0.9 cl.

The owner wishes to reduce the mean volume dispensed.

A random sample of twelve 75 cl bottles are taken from a batch filled by the new machine and the volume of wine in each bottle is measured. The volumes were

    75.7   76.2   75.4   75.8   75.4   76.9
    76.4   75.5   76.1   76.8   76.7   76.5 cl.

Investigate, at the 5% significance level, whether the volume of wine dispensed has been reduced.

Solution

The important facts to note are:

We are testing whether the mean is still 76.4 cl or whether a decrease has occurred.

This means that **H₀** is $\mu = 76.4$ cl
           and **H₁** is $\mu < 76.4$ cl a **one-tailed** test.

The test is at the **5%** significance level.

The volumes are normally distributed with known standard deviation of 0.9 cl.

The hypothesis test is carried out as follows:

    H₀ $\mu = 76.4$ cl
    H₁ $\mu < 76.4$ cl $\alpha = 0.05$

From tables, the critical value is $z = -1.6449$ for this one-tailed test.

The sample mean, $\bar{x} = 76.11667$ cl, from a sample with $n = 12$.

The population standard deviation is known, $\sigma = 0.9$ cl.

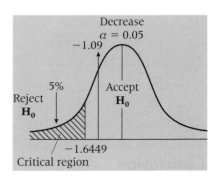

Therefore the test statistic

$$\frac{\bar{x} - \mu}{\frac{\sigma}{\sqrt{n}}} = \frac{76.11667 - 76.4}{\frac{0.9}{\sqrt{12}}} = -1.09$$

Conclusion

$-1.09 > -1.6449$ for this one-tailed test, hence $\mathbf{H_0}$ is accepted.

There is no significant evidence to suggest that the mean volume has decreased.

EXERCISE 3A

1 A factory produces lengths of rope for use in boatyards. The breaking strengths of these lengths of rope follow a normal distribution with a standard deviation of 4 kg.
The breaking strengths, in kg, of a random sample of 14 lengths of rope were as follows:

> 134　136　139　143　136　129　137
> 130　138　134　145　141　136　139.

The lengths of rope are intended to have a breaking strength of 135 kg but the manufacturer claims that the mean breaking strength is in fact greater than 135 kg.
Investigate the manufacturer's claim using a 5% level of significance.

2 Reaction times of adults in a controlled laboratory experiment are normally distributed with a standard deviation of 5 s.
Twenty-five adults were selected at random to take part in such an experiment and the following reaction times, in seconds, were recorded:

> 6.5　3.4　5.6　6.9　7.1　4.9　10.9　7.8
> 2.4　2.8　11.3　3.7　7.8　2.4　2.8　3.7
> 4.9　12.0　6.5　12.8　6.9　7.4　3.1　1.9　11.5

Investigate, using a 5% significance level, the hypothesis that the mean reaction time of adults is 7.5 s.

3 A maze is devised and after many trials, it is found that the length of time taken by adults to solve the maze is normally distributed with mean 7.4 s and standard deviation 2.2 s.
A group of nine children was randomly selected and asked to attempt the maze. Their times, in seconds, to completion were:

> 6.1　9.0　8.3　9.4　5.8　8.1　7.6　9.2　10.0

Assuming that the times for children are also normally distributed with a standard deviation of 2.2 s, investigate, using the 5% significance level, whether children take longer than adults to do the maze.

4 A machine produces steel rods which are supposed to be of length 2 cm. The lengths of these rods are normally distributed with a standard deviation of 0.02 cm.
A random sample of ten rods is taken from the production line and their lengths measured. The lengths are:

> 1.99　1.98　1.96　1.97　1.99　1.96　2.0　1.97　1.95　2.01 cm.

Investigate, at the 1% significance level, whether the mean length of rods is satisfactory.

5 The resistances, in ohms, of pieces silver wire follow a normal distribution with a standard deviation of 0.02 Ω.
A random sample of nine pieces of wire are taken from a batch and their resistances were measured with results:

1.53 1.48 1.51 1.48 1.54 1.52 1.54 1.49 1.51 Ω.

It is known that, if the wire is pure silver, the resistance should be 1.50 Ω but, if the wire is impure, the resistance will be increased.
Investigate, at the 5% significance level, whether the batch contains pure silver wire.

6 The weight of Venus chocolate bars is normally distributed with a mean of 30 g and a standard deviation of 3.5 g.
A random sample of 20 Venus bars was taken from the production line and was found to have a mean of 32.5 g. Is there evidence, at the 1% significance level, that the mean weight has increased?

7 The weights of components produced by a certain machine are normally distributed with mean 15.4 g and standard deviation 2.3 g.
The setting on the machine is altered and, following this, a random sample of 81 components is found to have a mean weight of 15.0 g.
Does this provide evidence, at the 5% level, of a reduction in the mean weight of components produced by the machine? Assume that the standard deviation remains unaltered.

8 The ability to withstand pain is known to vary from individual to individual.
In a standard test, a tiny electric shock is applied to the finger until a tingling sensation is felt. When this test was applied to a random sample of ten adults, the times recorded, in seconds, before they experienced a tingling sensation were:

4.2 4.5 3.9 4.4 4.1 4.5 3.7 4.8 4.2 4.2

Test, at the 5% level, the hypothesis that the mean time before an adult would experience a tingling sensation is 4.0 s. The times are known to be normally distributed with a standard deviation of 0.2 s.

3.6 Significance levels and problems to consider

You may have wondered how the **significance level** used in hypothesis testing is chosen. You have read that significance levels commonly used are 1%, 5% or 10% but no explanation has been offered about why this is so.

A common question asked by students is:

Why is the level of overwhelming evidence necessary to lead to rejection of H_0 commonly set at 5% ?

The **significance level** of a hypothesis test gives the P(test statistic lies inside critical region | H_0 true). In other words, *if* H_0 is true, then, with a 5% significance level, you would expect a result as extreme as this only once in every 20 times. If the test statistic does lie in the critical region the result is statistically significant at the 5% level and we conclude that H_0 is **untrue**.

Sometimes it may be necessary to be 'more certain' of a conclusion. If a traditional trusted piece of research is to be challenged, then a 1% level of significance may be used to ensure greater confidence in rejecting H_0.
If a new drug is to be used in preference to a well-known one then a 0.1% level may be necessary to ensure that no chance or fluke effects occur in research which leads to conclusions which may affect human health.

3.7 Errors

It is often quite a surprising concept for students to realise that, having correctly carried out a hypothesis test on carefully collected data and having made the relevant conclusion to accept the H_0 as true or to reject it as false, this conclusion might be right or it might be wrong.
However, you can never be absolutely certain that your conclusion is correct and has not occurred because of a *freak* result.
The significance level identifies for you the risk of a freak result leading to a wrong decision to reject H_0.
This leads many students to ask why tests so often use a **5% significance level** which has a probability of 0.05 of incorrectly rejecting H_0 when it actually is true. Why not reduce the significance level to 0.1% and then there would be a negligible risk of 0.001 of this error occurring?

The answer to this question comes from considering the **two** errors which may occur when conducting a hypothesis test. This table illustrates the problems:

		Conclusion	
		H_0 true	H_0 not true
Reality	H_0 correct	Conclusion correct	Error made **Type 1**
	H_0 incorrect	Error made **Type 2**	Conclusion correct

Not only can you conclude H_0 is true when really it is false but also you could conclude it is false when actually it is true.

The table shows that the **significance level** of a test is
P(conclusion H_0 not true | H_0 really is correct) =
P(**Type 1** error made).

The other error to consider is when a test does not show a
significant result even though the H_0 actually is **not** true.
P(conclusion H_0 true | H_0 really is incorrect)
= P(**Type 2** error made).

The probability of making a **Type 2** error is difficult or
impossible to evaluate unless precise further information is
available about values of the population parameters. If a value
suggested in H_0 is only slightly incorrect then there may be a
very high probability of making a **Type 2** error. If the value is
completely incorrect then the probability of a **Type 2** error will
be very small.

> You will not be expected to
> evaluate the probability of
> making a **Type 2** error in S4.

Obviously, if you set a very low **significance level** for a test,
then the probability of making a **Type 1** error will be low but
you may well have quite a high probability of making a **Type 2**
error.

There is no logical reason why 5% is used, rather than 4% or 6%.
However, practical experience over a long period of time has
shown that, in most circumstances, a significance level of 5%
gives a good balance between the risks of making **Type 1** and
Type 2 errors.

> If a low risk of wrongly rejecting
> H_0 is set, then it is unlikely that
> the test statistic will lie in the
> critical region. H_0 is unlikely to
> be rejected unless the null
> hypothesis is 'miles away' from
> reality.

This is why 5% is chosen as the 'standard' significance level for
hypothesis testing and careful consideration must be given
before changing this value.

> Errors which can occcur are:
> A **Type 1** error which is to reject H_0 when it is true.
> A **Type 2** error which is to accept H_0 when it is not true.

Worked example 3.4

A set of times, measured to one-hundredth of a second, were
obtained from nine randomly selected subjects taking part in a
psychology experiment.

The mean of the nine sample times was found to be 9.17 s.

It is known that these times are normally distributed with a
standard deviation of 4.25 s.

The hypothesis that the mean of such times is equal to 7.50 s is
to be tested, with an alternative hypothesis that the mean is
greater than 7.50 s, using a 5% level of significance.

Explain, in the context of this situation, the meaning of:

(a) a **Type 1** error,
(b) a **Type 2** error.

Solution

For this example:

H_0 $\mu = 7.50$ s
H_1 $\mu > 7.50$ s $\quad \alpha = 0.05$ one-tailed test.

(a) A **Type 1** error is to reject H_0 and conclude that the population mean time is **greater than** 7.50 s when, in reality, the mean time for such an experiment is equal to 7.50 s.

> If H_0 is untrue it is impossible to make a **Type 1** error.

The probability of this happening, if H_0 is true is $\alpha = 0.05$.

(b) A **Type 2** error is to accept H_0 and conclude that the population mean time is **equal to** 7.50 s when, in reality, the mean time for such an experiment is greater than 7.50 s.

> If H_0 is true it is impossible to make a **Type 2** error.

The probability of this happening will vary and can only be determined if more information is given regarding the exact alternative value that μ may take, not simply that $\mu > 7.50$ s.

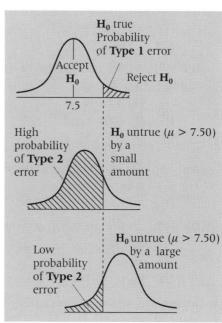

Worked example 3.5

Explain, in the context of Worked example 3.2, the meaning of:

(a) a **Type 1** error,
(b) a **Type 2** error.

Solution

In Worked example 3.2, we have:

H_0 $\mu = 11.5$ cm
H_1 $\mu \neq 11.5$ cm $\quad \alpha = 0.01$

Hence:

(a) A **Type 1** error is to reject H_0 and conclude that the mean growth of seedlings is **not equal** to 11.5 cm when, in reality, the mean growth for seedlings grown in the experimental soil preparation is equal to 11.5 cm.

The probability of this happening if H_0 is true is $\alpha = 0.01$.

(b) A **Type 2** error is to accept H_0 and conclude that the mean growth of seedlings is **equal** to 11.5 cm when, in reality, the mean growth for the seedlings grown in the experimental soil preparation is not equal to 11.5 cm.

As seen in the previous example, the probability of this cannot be determined unless precise information is given regarding the alternative value taken by μ.

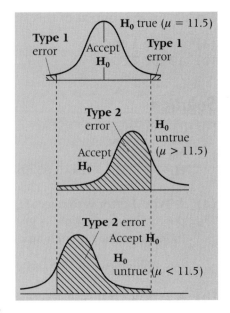

EXERCISE 3B

1 Refer to question 1 in Exercise 3A.

(a) Explain, in the context of this question, the meaning of:
   (i) a **Type 1** error,
   (ii) a **Type 2** error.

(b) What is the probability of making a **Type 1** error in this question if:
   (i) H_0 is true,
   (ii) H_0 is untrue?

2 Refer to question 4 in Exercise 3A.

(a) Explain, in the context of this question, the meaning of:
   (i) a **Type 1** error,
   (ii) a **Type 2** error.

(b) What is the probability of making a **Type 1** error in this question if:
   (i) H_0 is true,
   (ii) H_0 is untrue?

3 Times for glaze to set on pottery bowls follow a normal distribution with a standard deviation of three minutes. The mean time is believed to be 20 minutes.
A random sample of nine bowls is glazed with times which gave a sample mean of 18.2 minutes.

(a) Investigate, at the 5% significance level, whether the results of this sample support the belief that the mean glaze time is 20 minutes.

(b) Explain, in the context of this question, the meaning of a **Type 1** error.

(c) Why is it not possible to find the probability that a **Type 2** error is made?

4 The lengths of car components are normally distributed with a standard deviation of 0.45 mm. Ten components are selected at random from a large batch and their lengths were found to be,

> 19.3 20.5 18.1 18.3 17.6 19.0 20.1 19.2 18.6 19.4 mm.

(a) Investigate, at the 10% significance level, the claim that the mean length of such components is 19.25 mm.

(b) Explain, in the context of this question, the meaning of:

    (i) a **Type 1** error,

    (ii) a **Type 2** error.

(c) Write down the probability of making a **Type 1** error if the mean length is 19.25 mm.

5 A random sample of ten assembly workers in a large factory are trained and then asked to assemble a new design of electrical appliance. The times to assemble this appliance are known to follow a normal distribution with a standard deviation of 12 minutes. It is claimed that the new design is easier to assemble and the mean time should be less than the mean of 47 minutes currently taken to assemble the old design of appliance.
The mean time for the sample of ten workers was 39.8 minutes.

(a) Investigate, using a 5% significance level, the claim that the new design is easier to assemble.

(b) Explain, in the context of this question, the meaning of a **Type 2** error.

Key point summary

1 A hypothesis test needs two hypotheses identified at   *p46*
the beginning: H_0 the **Null Hypothesis** and H_1 the **Alternative Hypothesis**.

H_0 and H_1 both refer to the population from which the sample is randomly taken.

2 H_0 states that a situation is unchanged, that a   *p46*
population parameter takes its usual value.

H_1 states that the parameter has increased, decreased or just changed.

H_0 states what is to be assumed true unless overwhelming evidence proves otherwise. In the case of testing a mean, H_0 is $\mu = k$ for some suggested value of k.

60 Hypothesis testing

3 A **two-tailed** test is one where H_1 involves testing for any (non-directional) change in a parameter. *p47*

A **one-tailed** test is one where H_1 involves testing specifically for an increase or for a decrease (change in one direction only).

A **two-tailed test** results in a critical region with two areas.

A **one-tailed test** results in a critical region with one area.

4 The **critical region** or **critical value** identifies the range of extreme values which lead to the **rejection** of H_0. *p49*

The **critical value** is often found directly from statistical tables as in the case of testing a mean from a normally distributed population.

5 The **significance level**, α, of a test is the probability that a test statistic lies in the extreme critical region, if H_0 is true. It determines the level of overwhelming evidence deemed necessary for the rejection of H_0. *p49*

The **significance level**, α, is commonly, but not exclusively, set at 1%, 5% or 10%.

6 The general procedure for hypothesis testing is: *p49*
1 Write down H_0 and H_1
2 Decide which test to use
3 Decide on the significance level
4 Identify the critical region
5 Calculate the test statistic
6 Make your conclusion.

7 The **test statistic** used for investigating a hypothesis regarding the mean of a normally distributed population is, *p47*

$$\frac{\bar{x} - \mu}{\frac{\sigma}{\sqrt{n}}}$$

Where $\bar{x}$ is the mean of the randomly selected sample of size n and σ is the known population standard deviation.

If the **test statistic** lies **in** the **critical region**, or beyond the **critical value**, H_0 is rejected.

8 Errors which can occur are: *p56*
A **Type 1** error which is to reject H_0 when it is true.
A **Type 2** error which is to accept H_0 when it is not true.
The probability of making a **Type 1** error is usually denoted by α.

Test yourself	What to review
1 Which of the following hypotheses would require a one-tailed test and which a two-tailed test?	*Section 3.2*

1 Which of the following hypotheses would require a one-tailed test and which a two-tailed test?

(a) Amphetamines stimulate motor performance. The mean reaction time for those subjects who have taken amphetamine tablets will be slower than that for those who have not.

(b) The mean score on a new aptitude test for a precision job is claimed to be lower than the mean of 43 found on the existing test.

(c) Patients suffering from asthma have a higher mean health conscious index than people who do not suffer from asthma.

(d) The mean length of rods has changed since the overhaul of a machine.

Section 3.2

---

2 What is the name given to the value with which a test statistic is compared in order to decide whether a null hypothesis should be rejected?

Section 3.4

---

3 (a) What is the name given to the agreed probability of wrongly rejecting a null hypothesis?

(b) Give three commonly used levels for this probability.

Section 3.4

---

4 A manufacturer collects data on the annual maintenance costs for a random selection of eight new welding machines.
The mean cost of these eight machines is found to be £54.36.
The standard deviation of such costs for welding machines is £8.74.
Stating the null and alternative hypotheses, and using a 1% significance level, test whether there is any evidence that the mean cost for maintenance of the new machines is less than the mean value of £71.90 found for the old welding machines.

Section 3.5

---

5 In a survey of workers who travel to work at a large factory by car, the distances, in km, travelled by a random sample of ten workers were:

  14   43   17   52   22   25   68   32   26   44

In previous surveys, the mean distance was found to be 35.6 km with a standard deviation of 14.5 km.

(a) Investigate, using a 5% significance level, whether the mean distance travelled to work has changed. Assume the standard deviation remains 14.5 km.

(b) What is the meaning of:
  (i) a **Type 1** error,
  (ii) a **Type 2** error,
  in the context of this question?

(c) Why is it important that the sample of workers is selected at random from all those factory workers who travel to work by car?

Sections 3.3, 3.5 and 3.7

Test yourself ANSWERS

1 (a) one-tail; (b) one-tail; (c) one-tail; (d) two-tail.

2 Critical value.

3 (a) Significance level; (b) 1%, 5%, 10%.

4 ts −5.68 cv −2.3263 mean cost is less.

5 (a) ts −0.284 cv ±1.96 no change;
(b) (i) conclude there has been a change when in fact there has not,
(ii) conclude no change when in fact there has been a change;
(c) Conclusion unreliable if sample not random. For example, sample may have been taken only from white collar workers who may have a different mean travelling distance from manual workers.

CHAPTER 4

Further hypothesis testing for means

Learning objectives

After studying this chapter you should be able to:

■ test a hypothesis about a population mean based on a large sample
■ test a hypothesis about a population mean based on a sample from a normal population with an unknown standard deviation.

4.1 Hypothesis test for means based on a large sample from an unspecified distribution

As discussed in section 2.3, there are occasionally real life situations where we may wish to carry out a hypothesis test for a mean by examining a sample taken from a population where the standard deviation is known. However, it is much more likely that, if the mean of the population is unknown, the standard deviation will also be unknown. Provided that a large sample is available, then a sufficiently good estimate of the population standard deviation can be found from the sample. The use of a large sample also has the advantage that the sample mean is approximately normally distributed regardless of the distribution of the population.

> The definition of large is arbitrary but a sample size of $n \geq 30$ is usually considered 'large'.

> It is still important to ensure that the sample is randomly selected.

As in chapter 3, the **sample mean**, $\bar{x}$, is evaluated and, since this test involves a **large** sample, we know that the sample mean is approximately normally distributed. The standard deviation is also evaluated and used as an estimate of σ for this test.

The **test statistic** is $\dfrac{\bar{x} - \mu}{\frac{\sigma}{\sqrt{n}}}$ as before, and is compared to critical z values.

> As the sample is large it makes very little difference whether the divisor n or $n - 1$ is used when estimating σ. However as σ is being estimated from a sample it is correct to use the divisor $n - 1$.

To carry out a hypothesis test for a mean based on a **large** sample from an **unspecified** distribution:

the **test statistic** is $\dfrac{\bar{x} - \mu}{\frac{\sigma}{\sqrt{n}}}$.

An estimate of the standard deviation, σ, can be made from the sample, the **test statistic** is compared to **critical z values**. These are found in AQA Table 4.

Worked example 4.1

A manufacturer claims that the mean lifetime of her batteries is 425 hours. A competitor tests a random sample of 250 of these batteries and the mean lifetime is found to be 408 hours, with a standard deviation of 68 hours.

Investigate the claim of the competitor that the batteries have a mean lifetime less than 425 hours. Use a 1% significance level.

Solution

The important facts to note are:

We are testing whether the population mean lifetime is 425 hours or whether it is less than 425 hours.

This means that $\mathbf{H_0}$ is $\mu = 425$ hours
and $\mathbf{H_1}$ is $\mu < 425$ hours a **one-tailed** test.

The test is at the **1%** significance level.

The lifetimes are from an unspecified distribution with an unknown standard deviation. However, the sample size is **large** so $\bar{x}$ is approximately normally distributed and an estimate of the unknown population standard deviation can be calculated from the sample.

$n = 250.$

The hypothesis test is carried out as follows:

$\mathbf{H_0}$ $\mu = 425$ hours
$\mathbf{H_1}$ $\mu < 425$ hours $\quad \alpha = 0.01$

From tables, the critical value is $z = -2.3263$ for this one-tailed test.

The sample mean, $\bar{x} = 408$ hours, from a sample with $n = 250$.

The population standard deviation is estimated as $\sigma = 68$ hours.

The **test statistic** is $\dfrac{\bar{x} - \mu}{\dfrac{\sigma}{\sqrt{n}}} = \dfrac{408 - 425}{\dfrac{68}{\sqrt{250}}} = -3.95$

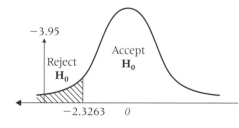

Conclusion

$-3.95 < -2.3263$ for this one-tailed test. Hence $\mathbf{H_0}$ is rejected.

There is significant evidence to suggest that the mean lifetime is less than the 425 hours claimed by the manufacturer.

Worked example 4.2

A precision machine is set to produce metal rods which have a mean length of 2 mm. A sample of 150 of these rods is randomly selected from the production of this machine. The sample mean is 1.97 mm and the standard deviation is 0.28 mm.

(a) Investigate, using the 5% significance level, the claim that the mean length of rods produced by the machine is 2 mm.

(b) How would your conclusions be affected if you later discovered that:

   (i) the sample was not random,

   (ii) the distribution was not normal?   [A]

Solution

(a) The important facts to note are:

We are testing whether or not the population mean length is 2 mm.

This is a **two-tailed** test.
The test is at the **5%** significance level.
The lengths are from an unspecified distribution with an unknown standard deviation. However, the sample size is **large**.
The hypothesis test is carried out as follows:

$$\mathbf{H_0}\ \mu = 2\ \text{mm}$$
$$\mathbf{H_1}\ \mu \neq 2\ \text{mm} \quad \alpha = 0.05$$

From tables, the critical value is $z = \pm 1.96$ for this two-tailed test.
The sample mean, $\bar{x} = 1.97$ mm, from a sample with $n = 150$.
The population standard deviation is estimated as $\sigma = 0.28$ mm.

The **test statistic** is $\dfrac{\bar{x} - \mu}{\dfrac{\sigma}{\sqrt{n}}} = \dfrac{1.97 - 2}{\dfrac{0.28}{\sqrt{150}}} = -1.31$

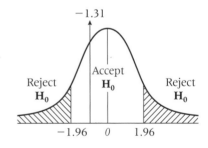

Conclusion

$-1.31 > -1.96$ for this two-tailed test. Hence $\mathbf{H_0}$ is accepted.

There is no significant evidence to suggest that a change in mean length has occurred.

We have shown that if $\mu = 2$ mm, a sample mean of 1.97 is not a particularly unlikely event.

(b) (i) If the sample was not random there can be no confidence in the conclusion. For example, these may have been the first 150 rods produced and the mean length could have changed as production continued.

    (ii) It makes no difference whether the distribution is normal or not as this is a large sample.

EXERCISE 4A

1 A factory produces lengths of cable for use in winches. These lengths are intended to have a mean breaking strength of 195 kg but the factory claims that the mean breaking strength is in fact greater than 195 kg.

In order to investigate this claim, a random sample of 80 lengths of cable is checked. The breaking strengths of these sample lengths are found to have a mean of 199.7 kg and a standard deviation of 17.4 kg. Carry out a suitable hypothesis test, using a 1% level of significance, to test the factory's claim.

2 The resistances, in ohms, of 5 mm pieces of wire for use in an electronics factory are supposed to have a mean of 1.5 Ω.

A random sample of 85 pieces of wire are taken from a large delivery and their resistances are carefully measured. Their mean resistance is 1.6 Ω and their standard deviation is 0.9 Ω. Investigate, at the 5% significance level, whether the mean resistance is 1.5 Ω.

3 A Government department states that the mean score of Year 2 children in a new national assessment test is 78%.

A large education authority selected 90 Year 2 children at random from all those who took this test in their area and found that the mean score for these children was 72.8%, with a standard deviation of 18.5%.

Investigate, using a 5% significance level, the hypothesis that the mean score of children in this area is lower than 78%.

4 A large dairy company produces whipped spread which is packaged into 500 g plastic tubs. Sixty tubs were randomly selected from the production line and weighed. The mean weight of these tubs was found to be 504 g with a standard deviation of 17.3 g.

Investigate, using the 5% significance level, whether the mean weight of the tubs is greater than 500 g.

5 A machine produces steel rods which are supposed to be of length 30 mm. A customer suspects that the mean length of the rods is less than 30 mm. The customer selects 50 rods from a large batch and measures their lengths.

The mean length of the rods in this sample was found to be 29.1 mm with a standard deviation of 2.9 mm.

Investigate, at the 1% significance level, whether the customer's suspicions are correct.

What assumption was it necessary to make in order to carry out this test?

6 The weight of Bubbles biscuit bars is meant to have a mean of 35 g.
A random sample of 120 Bubbles bars is taken from the production line and it is found that their mean weight is 36.5 g. The standard deviation of the sample weights is 8.8 g. Is there evidence, at the 1% significance level, that the mean weight is greater than 35 g?

7 Varicoceles is a medical condition in adolescent boys which may lead to infertility. A recent edition of *The Lancet* reported a study from Italy which suggested that the presence of this condition may be detected using a surgical instrument. The instrument gives a mean reading of 7.4 for adolescent boys who do not suffer from varicoceles. A sample of 73 adolescent boys who suffered from varicoceles gave a mean reading of 6.7 and a standard deviation of 1.2.

(a) Stating your null and alternative hypotheses and using a 5% significance level, investigate whether the mean reading for all adolescent boys who suffer from varicoceles is less than 7.4.

(b) Making reference to the value of your test statistic, comment briefly on the strength of the conclusion you have drawn.

(c) State, and discuss the validity of, any assumptions you have made in **(a)** about the method of sampling and about the distribution from which the data were drawn. [A]

4.2 Hypothesis test for means based on a sample from a normal distribution with an unknown standard deviation

This is a similar situation to that encountered in section 4.1 except for the fact that the sample is **not** large. Notice also that the sample is taken from a population which is known to be normally distributed.

For large samples it was not of great importance whether the divisor n or $n-1$ is used when calculating the standard deviation. Now, since the sample is not large, it is essential to use

$$s = \sqrt{\frac{\Sigma(x-\bar{x})^2}{n-1}}$$ as an estimate of σ.

There is some uncertainty in using s to estimate σ when a small sample is involved. The **t distribution** tables are used to find the critical values, rather than the normal distribution tables.

The test statistic is identical to that introduced in section 3.3, except for the fact that s, the estimated population standard deviation, is used instead of σ, the known population standard deviation.

The **test statistic** is $\dfrac{\bar{x} - \mu}{\frac{s}{\sqrt{n}}}$.

It is necessary to know the **degrees of freedom** before the critical value can be found. In section 2.4, you saw that an estimate of σ from a sample of size n has $n - 1$ **degrees of freedom**.

For example, in a one-tailed test, for an increase, at the 5% significance level using a sample of size ten, the **critical t value** is **1.833**

   (n = 10 so the degrees of freedom, $\nu = 9$ and p = 0.95)

and in a two-tailed test at the 1% significance level using a sample of size 15, the **critical t values** are **±2.977**

   (n = 15 so the degrees of freedom, $\nu = 14$ and p = 0.995)

> In the same way as this was written in section 2.4,
> $$t_{\alpha, n-1} = t_{0.05, 9} = 1.833$$
> and
> $$t_{\frac{\alpha}{2}, n-1} = t_{0.005, 14} = 2.977.$$

> To carry out a hypothesis test for a mean based on a sample from a **normal** distribution with an **unknown** standard deviation:
>
> the **test statistic** is $\dfrac{\bar{x} - \mu}{\frac{s}{\sqrt{n}}}$ where s = $\sqrt{\dfrac{\Sigma(x - \bar{x})^2}{n - 1}}$.
>
> s is used to estimate σ.
>
> The **test statistic** is compared to **critical t values**. These are found in AQA Table 5. For a sample of size n, the degrees of freedom, $\nu = n - 1$.

Worked example 4.3

Carrots are put into cans at a large food packaging factory. The machine which puts the carrots into the cans is set so that the amount of carrots put in a can is normally distributed with a mean of 220.5 g.

The carrot packaging process is halted for two days whilst the machines have their annual overhaul. Following this overhaul, a sample of eight cans is randomly selected and the contents weighed. The weights, in grams, of carrots in each can are:

   224.5 217.3 222.9 219.7 223.1 221.5 225.2 221.4

Using a 10% significance level, investigate whether there has been a change in the mean contents of these cans of carrots since the machine was overhauled.

Solution

The important facts to note are:

We are testing whether or not the population mean weight has changed from 220.5 g.

This is a **two-tailed** test.

The test is at the **10%** significance level.

The weights are from a normal distribution with an unknown standard deviation. The sample size is **not** large.

The hypothesis test is carried out as follows:

H_0 $\mu = 220.5$ g
H_1 $\mu \neq 220.5$ g $\alpha = 0.10$

From tables, the critical values are $t = \pm 1.895$ for this two-tailed test.

From the sample data, $\bar{x} = 221.95$ g $s = 2.577$ g $n = 8$

The **test statistic** is $\dfrac{\bar{x} - \mu}{\dfrac{s}{\sqrt{n}}} = \dfrac{221.95 - 220.5}{\dfrac{2.577}{\sqrt{8}}} = 1.59$

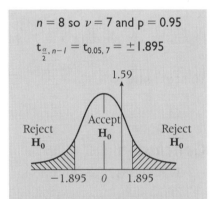

$n = 8$ so $\nu = 7$ and $p = 0.95$

$t_{\frac{\alpha}{2}, n-1} = t_{0.05, 7} = \pm 1.895$

Conclusion

$1.59 < 1.895$ for this two-tailed test. Hence H_0 is accepted.

There is no significant evidence to suggest that a change in mean weight of contents has occurred.

We have not **proved** that the true mean of the weight of carrots is 220.5 g, but there is no reason to doubt this if a sample of size eight has a mean of 221.95 g.

Worked example 4.4

Bottles of wine have nominal contents of 75 cl. The volumes of wine in bottles are normally distributed. It is suspected by a wine inspector that a particular vineyard is underfilling its wine bottles. The inspector takes a random sample of eleven bottles from the production of this vineyard and she measures the volume of wine in each bottle. The volumes, in centilitres, are found to be:

    75.12   72.67   74.37   73.22   75.91   73.28
    74.33   72.19   75.12   74.55   72.65

Carry out a test at the 5% significance level to investigate whether the mean volume of wine in a bottle is less than 75 cl.

Solution

The important facts to note are:

We are testing whether or not the population mean volume is less than 75 cl.

This is a **one-tailed** test.

The test is at the **5%** significance level.

The volumes are from a normal distribution with an unknown standard deviation. The sample size is **not** large.

The hypothesis test is carried out as follows:

H_0 $\mu = 75$ cl
H_1 $\mu < 75$ cl $\alpha = 0.05$

From tables, the critical value is $t = -1.812$ for this one-tailed test.

From the sample data, $\bar{x} = 73.946$ cl $s = 1.211$ cl $n = 11$

The **test statistic** is $\dfrac{\bar{x} - \mu}{\frac{s}{\sqrt{n}}} = \dfrac{73.946 - 75}{\frac{1.211}{\sqrt{11}}} = -2.89$

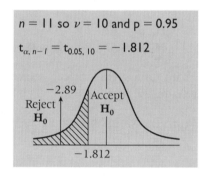

$n = 11$ so $\nu = 10$ and $p = 0.95$

$t_{\alpha, n-1} = t_{0.05, 10} = -1.812$

Conclusion

$-2.89 < -1.812$ for this one-tailed test. Hence H_0 is rejected.

There is significant evidence to suggest that the mean volume of wine in a bottle is less than 75 cl.

Worked example 4.5

The external diameter, in centimetres, of each of a random sample of 10 piston rings manufactured on a particular machine was measured as follows:

9.91   9.89   10.06   9.98   10.09
9.81   10.01   9.99   9.87   10.09

Stating any necessary assumption, test the claim that the piston rings manufactured on this machine have a mean external diameter of 10 cm. Use a 5% significance level.

Note that the question is asking you to state an assumption.

Solution

The important facts to note are:

We are testing whether or not the population diameter is equal to 10 cm.

This is a **two-tailed** test.

The test is at the **5%** significance level.

The diameters are from an **unspecified** distribution with an unknown standard deviation. The sample size is **not** large.

We must **assume** that the diameters are **normally distributed** in order for this test to be carried out using critical **t** values.

The hypothesis test is carried out as follows:

$$\mathbf{H_0}\ \mu = 10\ \text{cm}$$
$$\mathbf{H_1}\ \mu \neq 10\ \text{cm} \quad \alpha = 0.05$$

From tables, the critical value is **t** $= \pm 2.262$ for this two-tailed test.

From the sample data, $\bar{x} = 9.97$ cm $\quad s = 0.09695$ cm $\quad n = 10$

The **test statistic** is $\dfrac{\bar{x} - \mu}{\dfrac{s}{\sqrt{n}}} = \dfrac{9.97 - 10}{\dfrac{0.09695}{\sqrt{10}}} = -0.978$

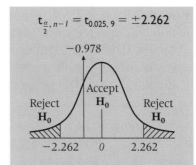

$$t_{\frac{\alpha}{2},\, n-1} = t_{0.025,\, 9} = \pm 2.262$$

Conclusion

$-0.978 > -2.262$ for this two-tailed test. Hence **H₀** is accepted.

There is no significant evidence to suggest that the mean is not 10 cm.

Again, we have not proved that the mean diameter is 10 cm. We just have no reason to doubt that assertion.

EXERCISE 4B

1 During a particular week, 13 babies were born in a maternity unit. Part of the standard procedure is to measure the length of the baby. Given below is a list of the lengths, in centimetres, of the babies born in this particular week.

   49 50 45 51 47 49 48 54 53 55 45 50 48

Assuming that this sample came from an underlying normal population, test, at the 5% significance level, the hypothesis that the population mean length is 50 cm.

2 The weights of steel ingots are known to be normally distributed. A random sample of 12 steel ingots is taken from a production line. The weights, in kilograms, of these ingots are given below.

   24.8   30.8   28.1   24.8   27.4   22.1
   24.7   27.3   27.5   27.8   23.9   23.2

Investigate the claim that the mean weight exceeds 25.0 kg using a 10% level of significance.

3 A random sample of 14 cows was selected from a large dairy herd at Brookfield Farm. Their milk yields are normally distributed. In one week the yields, in kilograms, for each cow are recorded. The results are given below.

169.6   142.0   103.3   111.6   123.4   143.5   155.1
101.7   170.7   113.2   130.9   146.1   169.3   155.5

Investigate the claim that the mean weekly milk yield for the herd is greater than 120 kg, using a 5% significance level.

4 A random sample of 15 workers from a vacuum flask assembly line was selected from a large number of such workers. Ivor Stopwatch, a work-study engineer, asked each of these workers to assemble a one litre vacuum flask at their normal working speed. The times taken, in seconds, to complete these tasks are given below.

109.2   146.2   127.9   92.0   108.5
 91.1   109.8   114.9   115.3   99.0
112.8   130.7   141.7   122.6   119.9

Assuming that this sample came from an underlying normal population, investigate the claim that the population mean assembly time is less than 2 minutes using a 5% significance level.

5 In processing grain in the brewing industry, the percentage extract recovered is measured. A brewer introduces a new source of grain and the percentage extract on 11 separate randomly selected days is as follows:

95.2   93.1   93.5   95.9   94.0   92.0
94.4   93.2   95.5   92.3   95.4

Test the hypothesis that the mean percentage extract recovered is 95.0 using a 5% significance level. What assumptions have you made in carrying out your test?

6 A car manufacturer introduces a new method of assembling a particular component. The old method had assembly times which were normally distributed with a mean of 42 minutes. The manufacturer would like the assembly time to be as short as possible, and so expects the new method to have a smaller mean. A random sample of assembly times (minutes) taken after the new method had become established was

27   39   28   41   47   42   35   32   38

Investigate the manufacturer's expectation using a 1% level of significance.

4.3 Mixed examples

In this and the previous chapter, you have been introduced to three separate sets of circumstances in which testing a mean, based on a randomly selected sample, may be carried out.

It is important to recognise which set of circumstances applies in any problem so that the correct test, either using the normal or Student's t distribution, is carried out.

It is also important to check whether the standard deviation of the population, σ, has been given and, if it has not, to ensure that the correct estimate for σ is used.

The following flow chart might help.

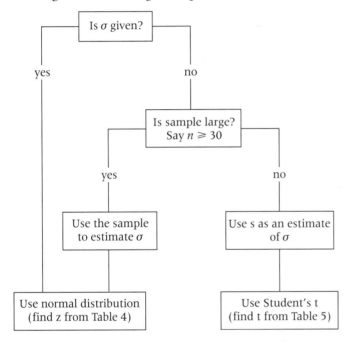

Some mixed examples are now given to illustrate how the decision making process for testing a mean works.

The mixed exercise following these examples covers different types of situations involved in testing a mean.

Worked example 4.6

A jam manufacturer produces thousands of pots of strawberry jam each week. The pots are filled by a machine such that the weights of jam delivered into the pots follow a normal distribution with mean 456 g and known standard deviation 0.7 g.

The manager of the factory feels that the mean is set too high and the machine is altered so that the mean should be reduced but the standard deviation remains unaltered.

Twelve pots of strawberry jam are taken at random from the production line following this adjustment. The amount of jam in each pot is measured with the following results in grams:

454.9 454.2 454.6 455.3 454.9 455.0
456.2 455.8 455.2 456.3 455.7 454.5

Investigate, using the 1% significance level, whether the adjustment has been satisfactory.

Solution

The important facts to note are:

We are testing whether or not the population mean weight is less than 456 g.

This is a **one-tailed** test.

The test is at the **1%** significance level.

The weights are from a **normal** distribution with a **known** standard deviation $\sigma = 0.7$ g.

The hypothesis test is carried out as follows, using the normal distribution and finding **z** from Table 4:

$\mathbf{H_0} \; \mu = 456$ g
$\mathbf{H_1} \; \mu < 456$ g $\alpha = 0.01$

From tables, the critical value is $\mathbf{z} = -2.3263$ for this one-tailed test.

From the sample data, $\bar{x} = 455.22$ g $n = 12$

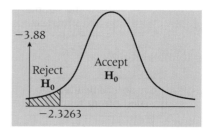

The **test statistic** is $\dfrac{\bar{x} - \mu}{\dfrac{\sigma}{\sqrt{n}}} = \dfrac{455.22 - 456}{\dfrac{0.7}{\sqrt{12}}} = -3.88$

Conclusion

$-3.88 < -2.3263$ for this one-tailed test. Hence $\mathbf{H_0}$ is rejected.

There is significant evidence to suggest that the mean weight of jam delivered by the machine is less than 456 g.

Worked example 4.7

A nurse decides to record how long his journey to work takes on 55 randomly chosen days over a period of one year since the construction of new dual carriageway was started. Before this long term construction was started, his mean journey time was 44.6 minutes.

The mean time found for the 55 journeys made during the construction period is 48.5 minutes with a standard deviation of 18.4 minutes.

Investigate, at the 5% significance level, whether the construction work has led to his mean journey time being increased.

Solution

The important facts to note are:

We are testing whether or not the population mean journey time has increased.

This is a **one-tailed** test.

The test is at the **5%** significance level.

The times are from an **unspecified** distribution with an unknown standard deviation. The sample size is **large**.

$n = 55.$

The hypothesis test is carried out as follows, using the normal distribution and finding z from Table 4:

H_0 $\mu = 44.6$ minutes
H_1 $\mu > 44.6$ minutes $\quad \alpha = 0.05$

From tables, the critical value is **z** $= 1.6449$ for this one-tailed test.

From the sample data,
$\bar{x} = 48.5$ minutes, the estimate of σ is 18.4 minutes, $n = 55$

The **test statistic** is $\dfrac{48.5 - 44.6}{\dfrac{18.4}{\sqrt{55}}} = 1.57$

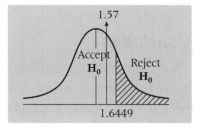

Conclusion

$1.57 < 1.6449$ for this one-tailed test. Hence H_0 is accepted.

There is no significant evidence to suggest that the mean journey time has increased.

Worked example 4.8

Industrial waste dumped in rivers reduces the amount of dissolved oxygen in the water. The mean dissolved oxygen content of samples of water taken from a river at a point just above a factory suspected of illegally dumping waste is 4.9 parts per million (ppm). The dissolved oxygen contents in ppm of samples of water taken from the river at a point below the factory were,

3.8   5.0   3.6   4.2   4.4   4.8   3.9   4.3   4.4.

(a) Stating clearly your null and alternative hypotheses, investigate at the 5% significance level whether the mean dissolved oxygen content is lower below the factory than above it. You should assume that the distribution is normal.

(b) On being shown the results the factory manager pointed out that there was a source of pollution (other than the factory) between the two points on the river which is known to reduce the dissolved oxygen content by 0.3 ppm. Does this further information affect your conclusions as to whether the factory is dumping waste or not? [A]

Solution

(a) The important facts to note are:

We are testing whether or not the population mean dissolved oxygen content is less than 4.9 ppm.

This is a **one-tailed** test.

The test is at the **5%** significance level.

The observations are from a **normal** distribution with an unknown standard deviation. The sample size is **not** large.

The hypothesis test is carried out as follows, using Student's t tables to find the critical value **t**:

$$\mathbf{H_0}\ \mu = 4.9$$
$$\mathbf{H_1}\ \mu < 4.9 \quad \alpha = 0.05$$

From tables, the critical value is **t** = −1.860 for this one-tailed test.

From the sample data, $\bar{x} = 4.2667 \quad s = 0.4555 \quad n = 9$

The **test statistic** is $\dfrac{\bar{x} - \mu}{\frac{s}{\sqrt{n}}} = \dfrac{4.2667 - 4.9}{\frac{0.4555}{\sqrt{9}}} = -4.17$

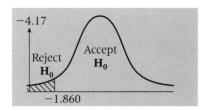

Conclusion

−4.17 < −1.860 Hence **H₀** is rejected.

There is significant evidence to suggest that dissolved oxygen content is less below the factory than above it and hence that the factory is dumping waste.

(b) With the known source of pollution we would expect the mean dissolved oxygen content to be 4.9 − 0.3 = 4.6 if the factory was not dumping waste.

The calculation is identical to **(a)** apart from the new hypotheses

$$\mathbf{H_0}\ \mu = 4.6$$
$$\mathbf{H_1}\ \mu < 4.6$$

The **test statistic** is $\dfrac{4.2667 - 4.6}{\frac{0.4555}{\sqrt{9}}} = -2.20$

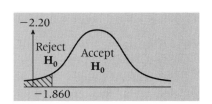

The critical value is unchanged at −1.860

The evidence that the factory is dumping waste is still significant.

MIXED EXERCISE

1 It is known that repeated weighings of the same object on a particular chemical balance give readings which are normally distributed.

Past evidence, using experienced operators, suggests that the mean is equal to the mass of the object and that the standard deviation is 0.25 mg. A trainee operator makes seven repeated weighings of the same object, which is known to have a mass of 19.5 mg, and obtains the following readings:

> 19.1   19.4   19.0   18.8   19.7   19.8   19.2

Investigate using the 5% significance level, whether the trainee operator's readings are biased.

Assume the standard deviation for the trainee operator is 0.25 mg.

2 A company produces high quality chocolates which are all in the shape of circular disks.

The diameters, in millimetres, of 19 randomly selected chocolates were,

> 279   263   284   277   281   269   266   271   262   275
> 266   272   281   274   279   277   267   269   275

(a) Assuming that the diameters of these chocolates are normally distributed, investigate, at the 10% significance level, the hypothesis that their mean diameter is 275 mm.

(b) What changes would you make to your test if it was known that the standard deviation of the diameters of these chocolates was 5 mm?

3 An investigation was conducted into the dust content in the flue gases of a particular type of solid-fuel boiler. Forty boilers were used under identical fuelling and extraction conditions. Over a given period, the quantities, in grams, of dust which was deposited in traps inserted in each of the forty flues were measured. The mean quantity for this sample of forty boilers was found to be 65.7 g, with a standard deviation of 2.9 g.

Investigate, at the 1% level of significance, the hypothesis that the population mean dust deposit is 60 g.

4 A large food processing firm is considering introducing a new recipe for its ice cream. In a preliminary trial, a panel of 15 tasters were each asked to score the ice cream on a scale from 0 (awful) to 20 (excellent). Their scores were as follows:

> 16   15   17   6   18   15   18   7   4   16   12   14   6   17   11

The scores in a similar trial for the firm's existing ice cream were normally distributed with mean 14 and standard deviation 2.2. Assuming that the new scores are also normally distributed with standard deviation 2.2, investigate whether the mean score for the new ice cream was lower than that of the existing one. Use a 5% significance level.

4

5 As part of a research project, a random sample of 11 students sat a proposed national Physics examination and obtained the following percentage marks:

> 30 44 49 50 63 38 43 96 54 40 26

Assuming such marks are normally distributed, investigate, using the 10% significance level, the hypothesis that the population mean examination mark is 40%.

6 The mean diastolic blood pressure for females is 77.4 mm. A random sample of 118 female computer operators each had their diastolic blood pressure measured. The mean diastolic blood pressure for this sample was 78.8 mm with a standard deviation of 7.1 mm. Investigate, at the 5% significance level, whether there is any evidence to suggest that female computer operators have a mean diastolic blood pressure higher than 77.4 mm.

7 The manager of a road haulage firm records the following times taken, in minutes, by a lorry to travel from the depot to a particular customer's factory.

> 43 35 47 180 39 58 40 39 51

The journey time of three hours was as a result of the driver being stopped by Customs & Excise Inspectors. The manager therefore removes this value before passing the data to you, as the firm's statistician, for analysis.

(a) Use the eight remaining values to investigate, at the 5% significance level, the hypothesis that the mean time for all journeys is 40 minutes.

(b) Comment on the manager's decision to remove the value of three hours and state what assumption may have been violated if this value had been included. [A]

8 Batteries supplied to a large institution for use in electric clocks had a mean working life of 960 days with a standard deviation of 135 days.

A sample from a new supplier had working lives of

> 1040 998 894 968 890
> 1280 1302 798 894 1350 hours.

Assume that the data may be regarded as a random sample from a normal distribution.

(a) Investigate whether the batteries from the new supplier have a longer working life than those from the original one. Use a 5% significance level and assume that the standard deviation of the batteries from the new supplier is also 135 days.

(b) If it cannot be assumed that the standard deviation of the batteries from the new supplier is still 135 days, explain how this would affect the test carried out in **(a)**.

(c) Carry out this new test and comment on your conclusions in **(a)** and **(c)**. [A]

9 A chamber of commerce claims that the average take-home pay of manual workers in full-time employment in its area is £140 per week. A sample of 125 such workers had mean take-home pay of £148 and standard deviation £28.

(a) Test, at the 5% significance level, the hypothesis that the mean take-home pay of all manual workers in the area is £140. Assume that the sample is random and that the distribution of take-home pay is normal. State clearly your null and alternative hypotheses.

(b) How would your conclusion be affected if you later discovered that:

(i) the distribution of take-home pay was not normal but the sample was random,

(ii) the sample was not random but the distribution of take-home pay was normal?

Give a brief justification for each of your answers. [A]

10 A pharmaceutical company claimed that a course of its vitamin tablets would improve examination performance. To publicise its claim, the company offered to provide the tablets free to candidates taking a particular GCSE examination. This offer was taken up by some but not all of the candidates. The average mark in the examination for all candidates who did not take the course of vitamin tablets was 42.0.

A random sample of 120 candidates from those who had taken the course of vitamin tablets gave a mean mark of 43.8 and a standard deviation of 12.8.

(a) Test, at the 5% significance level, whether the candidates who took the vitamin tablets had a mean mark greater than 42.0. State clearly your null and alternative hypotheses.

(b) Why was it not necessary to know that the examination marks were normally distributed before carrying out the test?

(c) Explain why, even if the mean mark of the sample had been much higher, the test could not prove that the course of vitamin tablets had improved examination performance. [A]

Key point summary

1 To carry out a hypothesis test for a mean based on   *p63*
   a **large** sample from an **unspecified** distribution:

   the **test statistic** is $\dfrac{\bar{x} - \mu}{\frac{\sigma}{\sqrt{n}}}$.

   An estimate of the standard deviation, σ, can be
   made from the sample, the **test statistic** is compared to
   critical z values. These are found in AQA Table 4.

2 To carry out a hypothesis test for a mean based on a   *p68*
   sample from a **normal** distribution with an **unknown**
   standard deviation:

   the **test statistic** is $\dfrac{\bar{x} - \mu}{\frac{s}{\sqrt{n}}}$ where $s = \sqrt{\dfrac{\Sigma(x - \bar{x})^2}{n - 1}}$.

   s is used to estimate σ.

   The **test statistic** is compared to **critical t values**. These
   are found in AQA Table 5. For a sample of size n, the degrees
   of freedom, $\nu = n - 1$.

Test yourself	What to review
1 What is the rule which is commonly used to determine whether a sample is **large**?	*Section 4.1*
2 When a population standard deviation is **unknown** and only a **small** sample is available, what is the name of the distribution which must be used in order to obtain the critical value for a test concerning the mean?	*Section 4.2*
3 State the degrees of freedom for a test concerning the mean based on a sample of size n.	*Section 4.2*
4 In each of the following cases find the critical value(s), if the hypotheses specified are tested at the 5% significance level:	*Section 4.3*

4

(a)
Sample mean	$\bar{x} = 32.6$
Sample size	$n = 250$
Null hypothesis	$\mathbf{H_0}\ \mu = 34$
Alternative hypothesis	$\mathbf{H_1}\ \mu \neq 34$
Population σ unknown	
Estimated standard deviation	$s = 17.6$
Population distribution unspecified	

(b)
Sample mean	$\bar{x} = 5.6$
Sample size	$n = 8$
Null hypothesis	$\mathbf{H_0}\ \mu = 5$
Alternative hypothesis	$\mathbf{H_1}\ \mu > 5$
Population σ unknown	
Estimated standard deviation	$s = 0.8$
Population has normal distribution	

(c)
Sample mean	$\bar{x} = 15.6$
Sample size	$n = 10$
Null hypothesis	$\mathbf{H_0}\ \mu = 17.5$
Alternative hypothesis	$\mathbf{H_1}\ \mu < 17.5$
Population σ unknown	
Estimated standard deviation	$s = 1.6$
Population has normal distribution	

(d)
Sample mean	$\bar{x} = 28.0$
Sample size	$n = 12$
Null hypothesis	$\mathbf{H_0}\ \mu = 30$
Alternative hypothesis	$\mathbf{H_1}\ \mu \neq 30$
Population standard deviation	$\sigma = 2.6$
Population has normal distribution	

5 Test the null hypothesis specified in question **4(b)** at the 1% significance level.	*Section 4.3*

Test yourself (*continued*)	What to review

6 Experimental components for use in aircraft engines were tested to destruction under extreme conditions. The survival times, X days, of ten components were as follows:

Section 4.2

207 381 411 673 534 294 597 344 418 554

(a) Investigate, at the 1% significance level, the claim that the mean survival time exceeds 400 days.

(b) What assumptions did you have to make in order to carry out the test in **(a)**?

(c) If you were told that evidence from past experience indicated that the population standard deviation of survival times is 101 days, what changes would you make to the test procedure in **(b)**?

(d) Carry out this modified test.

Test yourself **ANSWERS**

(d) ts 1.29   cv 2.326   accept mean does not exceed 400 days.

(c) use $\sigma = 101$ instead of s. Critical value from normal distribution instead of t;

(b) normal distribution, random sample;

6 (a) ts 0.898   cv 2.821   accept mean does not exceed 400 days;

5 ts 2.12   cv 2.998   accept $\mu = 5$.

4 (a) ∓1.96;   **(b)** 1.895;   **(c)** −1.833;   **(d)** ∓1.96.

3 $n − 1$.

2 t distribution.

1 n at least 30.

CHAPTER 5

Contingency tables

Learning objectives

After studying this chapter you should be able to:

- analyse contingency tables using the χ^2 distribution
- recognise the conditions under which the analysis is valid
- combine classes in a contingency table to ensure the expected values are sufficiently large
- apply Yates' correction when analysing 2×2 contingency tables.

5.1 Contingency tables

A biology student observed snails on a bare limestone pavement and in a nearby limestone woodland. The colour of each snail was classified as light, medium or dark.

The following table shows the number of snails observed in each category.

	Light	Medium	Dark
Pavement	22	10	3
Woodland	8	10	12

A table, such as the one above, which shows the frequencies of two variables (colour and habitat) simultaneously is called a contingency table.

> A contingency table shows the frequencies of two (or more) variables simultaneously.

It is possible for contingency tables to show the frequencies of more than two variables. In this module you will only meet tables showing two variables.

Contingency tables are analysed to test the null hypothesis that the two variables are independent. That is, in this case, that the proportion of light snails is the same in the woodland as on the limestone pavement as are the proportions of medium snails and of dark snails. Clearly the observed proportions are not the same – for example, a much larger proportion of light snails were observed on the pavement than in the woodland. However, (as in all hypothesis testing) the hypothesis refers to the population and the test is carried out to examine whether the observed sample could reasonably have occurred by chance if the null hypothesis was true.

To carry out the test, first calculate the expected number of snails you would observe in each category if the null hypothesis were true. To do this it is helpful to extend the table to include totals and sub-totals.

	Light	Medium	Dark	Total
Pavement	22	10	3	35
Woodland	8	10	12	30
Total	30	20	15	65

> row totals

grand total

column totals

The table now shows the totals for each row and for each column (the sub-totals). It also shows the total number of snails observed.

If there are the same proportion of light snails on the pavement as in the woodland then the best estimate that can be made of this proportion is the total number of light snails observed divided by the total number of snails observed. That is $\frac{30}{65}$.

Since a total of 35 snails was observed on the pavement you would expect to observe $\left(\frac{30}{65}\right) \times 35 = 16.15$ light snails on the pavement.

The expected number refers to a long run average and so will usually not be a natural number.

Similarly you would expect $\left(\frac{30}{65}\right) \times 30$ light snails to have been observed in the woodland, $\left(\frac{20}{65}\right) \times 35$ medium snails to have been observed on the pavement, etc.

This formula works for all contingency tables providing you are investigating the independence of two variables.

Notice that in each case the expected number in a particular cell is $\dfrac{\text{(row total)} \times \text{(column total)}}{\text{(grand total)}}$.

> The expected number in any cell of a contingency table is $\dfrac{\text{(row total)} \times \text{(column total)}}{\text{(grand total)}}$.

The following table shows the observed number, O, on the left of each cell and the expected number, E, on the right of each cell.

	Light	Medium	Dark	Total
Pavement	22, 16.15	10, 10.77	3, 8.08	35
Woodland	8, 13.85	10, 9.23	12, 6.92	30
Total	30	20	15	65

It is usually sufficient to calculate the *E*s to two decimal places. However the more significant figures used at this stage of the calculation the better.

Note that the total of the *E*s is the same as the total of the *O*s in each row and in each column. In this case it was only necessary to derive two Es – say for the expected number of Light and Medium snails observed on the pavement – and the rest could have been deduced from the totals.

The test statistic is $X^2 = \Sigma \dfrac{(O - E)^2}{E}$. This will have a small value if the observed frequencies in each cell are close to the frequencies expected. It will have a large value if there are big differences between the frequencies observed and those expected. Hence the null hypothesis will be accepted if $X^2 = \Sigma \dfrac{(O - E)^2}{E}$ is small and rejected if it is large.

The test statistic X^2 is approximately distributed as a χ^2 distribution provided the Os are frequencies (i.e. not lengths, weights, percentages, etc.) and the Es are reasonably large (say >5). Note the contingency table must also be complete. For example, it would not be permissible to leave the dark snails out of the analysis of the contingency table above.

> $X^2 = \Sigma \dfrac{(O - E)^2}{E}$ may be approximated by the χ^2 distribution
> provided:
> **(i)** the Os are frequencies,
> **(ii)** the Es are reasonably large, say >5.

To obtain a critical value from the χ^2 distribution it is necessary to know the degrees of freedom. General rules exist for deriving degrees of freedom but in the case of an $m \times n$ contingency table all you need to know is that the number of degrees of freedom is $(m - 1)(n - 1)$.

> An $m \times n$ contingency table has $(m - 1)(n - 1)$ degrees of freedom.

The contingency table above is 2×3 and so there are

$(2 - 1)(3 - 1) = 2$ degrees of freedom.

Note that 2 was also the number of Es which had to be derived from the null hypothesis before the rest could be calculated from the totals. This is not a coincidence and is one way of interpreting degrees of freedom.

The analysis of the contingency table can now be completed.

	Light	Medium	Dark	Total
Pavement	22, 16.15	10, 10.77	3, 8.08	35
Woodland	8, 13.85	10, 9.23	12, 6.92	30
Total	30	20	15	65

Side notes:

X^2 is used as it is similar but not identical to χ^2. There is no universally recognised symbol for this statistic.

For the analysis to be valid it must be possible to allocate each snail examined to one and only one cell.

5

Alternatively, note that once the sub-totals are known there are only two independent frequencies. Once these are known the rest are fixed.

H_0 Colour is independent of whether a snail is found on limestone pavement or in woodland.
H_1 Colour is not independent of whether a snail is found on limestone pavement or in woodland.

$$X^2 = \Sigma \frac{(O - E)^2}{E} = \frac{(22 - 16.15)^2}{16.15} + \frac{(10 - 10.77)^2}{10.77}$$

$$+ \frac{(3 - 8.08)^2}{8.08} + \frac{(8 - 13.85)^2}{13.85}$$

$$+ \frac{(10 - 9.23)^2}{9.23} + \frac{(12 - 6.92)^2}{6.92}$$

$$= 11.6$$

You may prefer to set the calculation out in a table

O	E	$\dfrac{(O - E)^2}{E}$
22	16.15	2.1190
10	10.77	0.0551
3	8.08	3.1939
8	13.85	2.4709
10	9.23	0.0642
12	6.92	3.7292

$$X^2 = \Sigma \frac{(O - E)^2}{E} = 11.6$$

The Os are frequencies and the Es are all greater than five and so we can compare the calculated value of X^2 with a critical value from the χ^2 distribution. The degrees of freedom as calculated above are $(2 - 1)(3 - 1) = 2$.

> The test will be one-tailed since a small value of X^2 indicates good agreement between Os and Es. Only a large value of X^2 will lead to H_0 being rejected.

Table 6 Percentage points of the χ^2 distribution

The table gives the values of x satisfying $P(X \leqslant x) = p$, where X is a random variable having the χ^2 distribution with ν degrees of freedom.

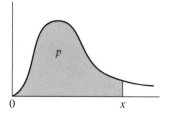

ν	p 0.005	0.01	0.025	0.05	0.1	0.9	0.95	0.975	0.99	0.995	ν p
1	0.00004	0.0002	0.001	0.004	0.016	2.706	3.841	5.024	6.635	7.879	1
2	0.010	0.020	0.051	0.103	0.211	4.605	5.991	7.378	9.210	10.597	2
3	0.072	0.115	0.216	0.352	0.584	6.251	7.815	9.348	11.345	12.838	3
4	0.207	0.297	0.484	0.711	1.064	7.779	9.488	11.143	13.277	14.860	4

For a 5% significance level the critical value is 5.991. Since $X^2 = 11.6$ and exceeds 5.991, H_0 is rejected and we conclude that the colour is not independent of where the snail was found. This is all that can be concluded from the hypothesis test. However, if the null hypothesis is rejected, an examination of the table will usually suggest some further interpretation which will make the result more informative. In this case the table suggests that snails found on the pavement tend to be lighter coloured than those found in the woodland.

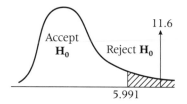

More light snails were observed than were expected on the pavement.

Worked example 5.1

In 1996 Prestbury School entered 45 candidates for A level statistics, while Gorton School entered 34 candidates. The following table summarises the grades obtained.

	A or B	C or D	E	N or U
Prestbury School	8	18	11	8
Gorton School	16	8	5	5

(a) Test at the 5% significance level whether the grades obtained are independent of the school.

(b) Which school has the better results? Explain your answer.

(c) Give two reasons why the school with the better results may not be the better school. [A]

Solution

(a) H_0 grades obtained are independent of school
H_1 grades obtained not independent of school

The following table shows in, each cell, the observed number on the left-hand side and the expected number (assuming the null hypothesis is true) on the right-hand side. For example the expected number obtaining A or B grades at Prestbury school is $\dfrac{45 \times 24}{79} = 13.67$

	A or B	C or D	E	N or U	Total
Prestbury School	8, 13.67	18, 14.81	11, 9.11	8, 7.41	45
Gorton School	16, 10.33	8, 11.19	5, 6.89	5, 5.59	34
Total	24	26	16	13	79

$$X^2 = \Sigma \frac{(O - E)^2}{E} = \frac{(8 - 13.67)^2}{13.67} + \frac{(18 - 14.81)^2}{14.81}$$

$$+ \frac{(11 - 9.11)^2}{9.11} + \frac{(8 - 7.41)^2}{7.41}$$

$$+ \frac{(16 - 10.33)^2}{10.33} + \frac{(8 - 11.19)^2}{11.19}$$

$$+ \frac{(5 - 6.89)^2}{6.89} + \frac{(5 - 5.59)^2}{5.59}$$

$$= 8.08$$

> The Es have been rounded to 2 dp. Despite this the calculated value of X^2 is correct to 3 sf.

The Os are frequencies and the Es are all greater than five and so we can compare the calculated value of X^2 with a critical value from the χ^2 distribution.

This is a 2×4 contingency table and so the degrees of freedom are $(2 - 1)(4 - 1) = 3$.

For a 5% significance level the critical value is 7.815.

H_0 is rejected and we conclude that the grades obtained are not independent of the school.

> Don't forget the test is one-tailed.

(b) From the table you can see that Prestbury school got less A or B grades than expected and more of the lower grades than expected. Gorton school got more A or B grades than expected and less of the lower grades than expected. The hypothesis test shows that this is unlikely to have occurred by chance and so you can conclude that Gorton school had the better results.

(c) A level results are only one aspect of a school's worth and cannot on their own be used as a measure of how good a school is. The analysis takes no account of the different intakes of the two schools.

Worked example 5.2

In 1996 Ardwick School entered 130 candidates for GCSE of whom 70% gained five or more passes at grade C or above. The figures for Bramhall School were 145 candidates of whom 60% gained five or more passes at grade C or above, and for Chorlton School were 120 candidates of whom 65% gained five or more passes at grade C or above.

Form these data into a contingency table and test whether the proportion of candidates obtaining five or more passes at grade C or above is independent of the school.

Solution

A contingency table must show frequencies, not percentages and the classes must not overlap. Thus for each school it is necessary to calculate the number of candidates who gained five or more passes at grade C and above and the number of candidates who did not do so.

For Ardwick school $\dfrac{70 \times 130}{100} = 91$ candidates gained five or

more passes at grade C and above and $130 - 91 = 39$ did not.

Similarly for Bramhall school $\dfrac{60 \times 145}{100} = 87$ did and

$145 - 87 = 58$ did not and for Chorlton school $\dfrac{65 \times 120}{100} = 78$ did and $120 - 78 = 42$ did not.

	Ardwick	Bramhall	Chorlton
5 or more passes	91	87	78
<5 passes	39	58	42

H_0 passing five or more GCSEs at grade C is independent of school
H_1 passing five or more GCSEs at grade C is not independent of school

The following table shows in, each cell, the observed number on the left-hand side and the expected number (assuming the null hypothesis is true) on the right-hand side. For example, the expected number obtaining five or more GCSE pass grades at Ardwick school is $\dfrac{256 \times 130}{395} = 84.25$.

	Ardwick	Bramhall	Chorlton	Total
5 or more passes	91, 84.25	87, 93.97	78, 77.77	256
<5 passes	39, 45.75	58, 51.03	42, 42.23	139
Total	130	145	120	395

$$X^2 = \Sigma \frac{(O - E)^2}{E} = 3.01$$

The Os are frequencies and the Es are all greater than five and so we can compare the calculated value of X^2 with a critical value from the χ^2 distribution. This is a 2×3 contingency table and so the degrees of freedom are $(2 - 1)(3 - 1) = 2$.

For a 5% significance level the critical value is 5.991. Hence the null hypothesis is accepted and we conclude that there is no convincing evidence to show a difference in the proportions obtaining five or more GCSEs at grade C at the three schools.

> If the table showed, for each school, the total candidates and the number who gained five or more passes at grade C, it would contain the same information but it would not be a contingency table.

5

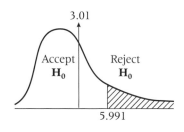

EXERCISE 5A

1 A dairy farmer kept a record of the time of delivery of each calf and the type of assistance the cow needed. Part of the data is summarised below.

	Day	Night
Unattended	42	58
Farmer assisted	63	117
Supervised by a vet	85	35

Investigate, at the 1% significance level, whether there is an association between time of day and type of birth.

2 In a survey on transport, electors from three different areas of a large city were asked whether they would prefer money to be spent on general road improvement or on improving public transport. The replies are shown in the following contingency table:

	Area		
	A	B	C
Road improvement preferred	22	46	24
Public transport preferred	78	34	36

Test, at the 1% significance level, whether the proportion favouring expenditure on general road improvement is independent of the area.

3 A statistics conference, lasting four days, was held at a university. Lunch was provided and on each day a choice of a vegetarian or a meat dish was offered for the main course. Of those taking lunch, the uptake was as follows:

	Tuesday	Wednesday	Thursday	Friday
vegetarian	17	24	21	16
meat	62	42	38	22

Test at the 5% significance level, whether the choice of dish for the main course was independent of the day of the week.

4 A survey into women's attitudes to the way in which women are portrayed in advertising was carried out for a regional television company to provide background information for a discussion programme. A questionnaire was prepared and interviewers approached women in the main shopping areas of Manchester and obtained 567 interviews.

(a) Explain why the women interviewed could not be regarded as a random sample of women living in the Manchester area.

(b) The respondents were classified by age and the following table gives the number of responses to the question 'Do you think that the way women are generally portrayed in advertising is degrading?'

	Under 35 years	35 years and over
yes definitely	85	70
yes	157	126
no	48	11
definitely not	12	3
no opinion or don't know	34	21

Use a χ^2 test, at the 5% significance level, to test whether respondents' replies are independent of age. [A]

5 A private hospital employs a number of visiting surgeons to undertake particular operations. If complications occur during or after the operation the patient has to be transferred to the NHS hospital nearby where the required back-up facilities are available.

A hospital administrator, worried by the effects of this on costs examines the records of three surgeons. Surgeon A had six out of her last 47 patients transferred, surgeon B four out of his last 72 patients, and surgeon C 14 out of his last 41.

(a) Form the data into a 2×3 contingency table and test, at the 5% significance level, whether the proportion transferred is independent of the surgeon.

(b) The administrator decides to offer as many operations as possible to surgeon B. Explain why and suggest what further information you would need before deciding whether the administrator's decision was based on valid evidence. [A]

6 The following table gives the number of candidates taking AEB Advanced Level Mathematics (Statistics) in June 1984, classified by sex and grade obtained.

	Grade obtained		
	A,B or C	D or E	O or F
Male	529	304	496
Female	398	223	271

In 1984 candidates who just failed to obtain grade E were awarded an O level. Those failing to achieve this were graded F.

(a) Use the χ^2 distribution and a 1 % significance level to test whether sex and grade obtained are independent.

(b) Which sex appears to have done better? Explain your answer.

(c) The following table gives the percentage of candidates in the different grades for all the candidates taking Mathematics (Statistics) and for all the candidates taking Mathematics (Pure and Applied) in June 1984.

	Percentage of candidates		
	A, B or C	D or E	O or F
Mathematics (Statistics)	41.5	23.8	34.7
Mathematics (Pure and Applied)	29.2	26.2	44.6

(i) Explain what further information is needed before a 3×2 table can be formed from which the independence of subject and grade can be tested.

(ii) When such a table was formed the calculated value of $\Sigma \dfrac{(O - E)^2}{E}$ was 131.6. Carry out the test using a 0.5% significance level.

(iii) Discuss, briefly, whether this information indicates that it is easier to get a good grade in 'Statistics' than in 'Pure and Applied'. [A]

7 Analysis of the rate of turnover of employees by a personnel manager produced the following table showing the length of stay of 200 people who left a company for other employment.

Grade	Length of employment (years)		
	0–2	2–5	>5
Managerial	4	11	6
Skilled	32	28	21
Unskilled	25	23	50

> This is a 3×3 table. The Es are calculated from the sub-totals in exactly the same way as in the previous examples.

Using a 1% level of significance, analyse this information and state fully your conclusions.

5.2 Small expected values

If the expected values are small then although it is still possible to calculate $\Sigma \dfrac{(O - E)^2}{E}$ it is no longer valid to obtain a critical value from the χ^2 distribution. This problem can usually be overcome by combining classes together to increase the expected values. There are three main points bear in mind when considering this procedure:

> This is because if E is small, a small difference between O and E can lead to a relatively large value of $\dfrac{(O - E)^2}{E}$.

- It is the expected values, E, which should be reasonably large; small observed values, O, do not cause any problem
- The classes must be combined in such a way that the data remains a contingency table
- In order to be able to interpret the conclusions, classes with small Es should be combined with the most similar classes.

> A rule of thumb is that all Es should be greater than five.

> Having decided to combine classes look at the nature of the classes **not** the size of the Es in other classes.

If it is necessary to combine classes to increase the size of the Es, the most similar classes should be combined.

Worked example 5.3

A University requires all entrants to a science course to study a non-science subject for one year. The non-science subjects available and the number of students of each sex studying them are shown in the table below.

	French	Poetry	Russian	Sculpture
Male	2	8	15	10
Female	10	17	21	37

Use a χ^2 test at the 5% significance level to test whether choice of subject is independent of gender.

Solution

H$_0$ choice of subject is independent of gender
H$_1$ choice of subject is not independent of gender

Calculating the expected values in the usual way and writing them on the right-hand side of each cell gives the following table:

	French	Poetry	Russian	Sculpture	Total
Male	2, 3.50	8, 7.29	15, 10.50	10, 13.71	35
Female	10, 8.50	17, 17.71	21, 25.50	37, 33.29	85
Total	12	25	36	47	120

> As there is only one small E and it is only a little less than five this is a borderline case. However it is safer to stick to the rule that all Es should be greater than five.

The expected value for males taking French is less than five. Choose the most similar subject to combine this with. In this case Russian is clearly the appropriate choice as it is the only other language. (We cannot just combine the French and Russian for males as this would leave three cells for males and four cells for females and there would no longer be a contingency table.)

The amended table is as follows:

	Language	Poetry	Sculpture	Total
Male	17, 14.00	8, 7.29	10, 13.71	35
Female	31, 34.00	17, 17.71	37, 33.29	85
Total	48	25	47	120

$$X^2 = \Sigma \frac{(O - E)^2}{E} = 2.42$$

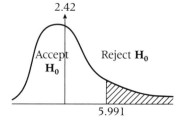

There are two degrees of freedom and for a 5% significance level the critical value is 5.991. Hence the null hypothesis is accepted and we conclude that there is no convincing evidence to show a difference in the choices of males and females.

Worked example 5.4

A small supermarket chain has a branch in a city centre and also at an out-of-town shopping centre eight miles away. An investigation into the mode of transport used to visit the stores by a random sample of shoppers yielded the data below.

	Mode of transport			
	Bicycle	Public transport	Private car/taxi	Walk
City centre branch	6	20	36	8
Out-of-town branch	2	9	40	1

(a) **(i)** Investigate, at the 5% significance level, whether the mode of transport is independent of the branch.

(ii) Describe any differences in the popularity of the different modes of transport used to visit the two branches.

The supermarket chain now extends the investigation and includes data from all of its 14 branches. A 4×14 contingency table is formed and the statistic

$$\Sigma \frac{(O - E)^2}{E}$$

is calculated correctly as 56.2 with no grouping of cells being necessary.

(b) Investigate the hypothesis that the mode of transport is independent of the branch:

(i) using a 5% significance level,

(ii) using a 1% significance level.

(c) Compare and explain the conclusions you have reached in **(b) (i)** and **(ii)**. [A]

Solution

(a) (i) H_0 mode of transport is independent of branch
H_1 mode of transport is not independent of branch

Calculating the expected values in the usual way and writing them on the right-hand side of each cell gives the following table.

	Mode of transport				
	Bicycle	**Public transport**	**Private car/taxi**	**Walk**	**Total**
City centre	6, 4.59	20, 16.64	36, 43.61	8, 5.16	70
Out-of-town	2, 3.41	9, 12.36	40, 32.39	1, 3.84	52
Total	8	29	76	9	122

The expected numbers going by bicycle to each branch are below five. The most similar form of transport to cycling is walking since both are self-propelled. Fortunately combining cycling and walking also eliminates the problem of the expected number walking to the out-of-town branch being less than five.

The table now becomes

	Mode of transport			
	Bicycle/ Walk	**Public transport**	**Private car/taxi**	**Total**
City centre	14, 9.75	20, 16.64	36, 43.61	70
Out-of-town	3, 7.25	9, 12.36	40, 32.39	52
Total	17	29	76	122

$$X^2 = \Sigma\frac{(O - E)^2}{E} = 9.05$$

There are two degrees of freedom and for a 5% significance level the critical value is 5.991. Hence the null hypothesis is rejected and we conclude that the method of transport is not independent of branch.

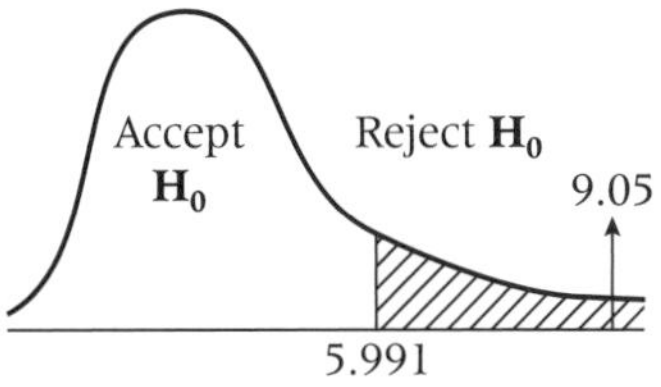

(ii) Examining the table it can be seen that at the city centre branch the observed value for bicycle/walk and for public transport exceeded the expected values whereas the observed value for Private car/taxi was less than expected. It therefore appears that private cars or taxis are less likely to be used when visiting the city centre branch than when visiting the out-of-town branch.

(b) **(i)** The expected values for a 4 × 14 contingency table are calculated in exactly the same way as in any of the tables above. There are $(4 - 1)(14 - 1) = 39$ degrees of freedom. Using a 5% significance level the critical value is 54.572 which is less than 56.2 and so we would conclude that mode of transport is not independent of branch.

> You have been given the value of X^2 as there would not be time in an examination to calculate the Es for such a large table.

(ii) Using a 1% significance level the critical value is 62.428 which is greater than 56.2 and so we would accept that the mode of transport is independent of branch.

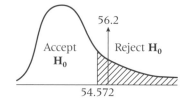

(c) The conclusions in **(b)** mean that if you are prepared to accept a 5% risk of claiming that mode of transport is not independent of branch when in fact it is independent of branch, then you can conclude that mode of transport is not independent of branch. If however you are only prepared to accept a 1% risk, there is insufficient evidence to conclude that mode of transport is not independent of branch.

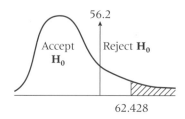

EXERCISE 5B

1 A market researcher is required to interview residents of small villages, aged 18 years and over. She has been allocated a quota of 50 males and 80 females. The age and sex distribution of the her interviewees are summarised below.

Age Group	Male	Female
18–29	3	5
30–39	29	21
40–49	13	40
60 and over	5	14

Investigate, using a 5% significance level, whether there is an association between the sex and age of her interviewees.

2 A manufacturer of decorating materials shows a panel of customers five different colours of paint and asks each one to identify their favourite. The choices classified by sex are shown in the table below.

	White	Pale green	Red	Dark green	Black
male	8	2	32	9	8
female	14	5	24	8	10

Test whether choice is independent of gender.

3 The number of communications received, during a particular week, by the editor of a local newspaper are shown in the table below. They have been classified by subject and by whether they were received by letter or by email.

	Politics	Football	Sport (other than football)	Miscellaneous
Letter	20	16	3	27
Email	15	8	2	10

Investigate, using a 1% significance level whether method of communication is associated with subject.

4 A survey is to be carried out among hotel guests to discover what features they regard as important when choosing an hotel. In a pilot study guests were asked to rate a number of features as important or not important. The results for four features are shown below (the number rating each feature is not the same, as not all guests were asked to rate the same features).

	Adequate lighting for reading in bed	Comfortable beds	Courteous staff	Squash courts available
important	28	34	26	4
not important	12	17	10	29

(a) Test, at the 5% significance level, whether the proportion of guests rating a feature important is independent of the feature.

(b) Comment on the relative importance of the four features.

(c) Under what circumstances would it be necessary to pool the results from more than one feature in order to carry out a valid test?

(d) If the results for 'adequate lighting for reading in bed' had to be pooled with another feature, which one would you choose and why?

(e) In the final survey 30 features were rated as unimportant, important or very important. The analysis of the resulting contingency table led to a value of 82.4 for $\sum \frac{(O-E)^2}{E}$ (no features were pooled). Test, at the 5% significance level, whether the rating was independent of the feature. [A]

5.3 Yates' correction for 2 × 2 contingency tables

Given the appropriate conditions $X^2 = \Sigma\dfrac{(O - E)^2}{E}$ can be approximated by a χ^2 distribution. In the case of a 2×2 contingency table the approximation can be improved by using $\Sigma\dfrac{(|O - E| - 0.5)^2}{E}$ instead of $\Sigma\dfrac{(O - E)^2}{E}$. This is known as Yates' correction.

> The underlying reason for this is that the Os are discrete but the χ^2 distribution is continuous. Hence this is often called Yates' continuity correction.

For a 2×2 table, $\Sigma\dfrac{(|O - E| - 0.5)^2}{E}$ should be calculated. This is known as Yates' correction.

> $|x|$ means the numerical value of x. Thus $|6| = 6$ and $|-3| = 3$.

Worked example 5.5

A university requires all entrants to a science course to study a non-science subject for one year. In the first year of the scheme entrants were given the choice of studying French or Russian. The number of students of each sex choosing each language is shown in the following table:

	French	Russian
Male	39	16
Female	21	14

Use a χ^2 test at the 5% significance level to test whether choice of language is independent of gender.

Solution

H$_0$ Subject chosen is independent of gender
H$_1$ Subject chosen is not independent of gender

Calculating expected values in the usual way and writing them in the right-hand side of the cell gives,

	French	Russian	Total
Male	39, 36.67	16, 18.33	55
Female	21, 23.33	14, 11.67	35
Total	60	30	90

	O	E	$O - E$	$\lvert O - E \rvert - 0.5$	$\dfrac{(\lvert O - E \rvert - 0.5)^2}{E}$
Male/French	39	36.67	2.33	1.83	0.091
Male/Russian	16	18.33	−2.33	1.83	0.183
Female/French	21	23.33	−2.33	1.83	0.144
Female/Russian	14	11.67	2.33	1.83	0.287

> Be careful to find the modulus of $O - E$ (i.e. $\lvert O - E \rvert$) **before** subtracting 0.5.

$$\sum \frac{(\lvert O - E \rvert - 0.5)^2}{E} = 0.705$$

There are $(2 - 1) \times (2 - 1) = 1$ degrees of freedom. Critical value for 5% significance level is 3.841.

Accept that choice of subject is independent of gender.

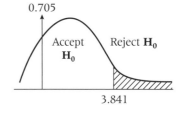

EXERCISE 5C

1 Two groups of patients took part in an experiment in which one group received an anti-allergy drug and the other group received a placebo. The following table summarises the results:

	Drug	Placebo
Allergies exhibited	24	29
Allergies not exhibited	46	21

Investigate, at the 5% significance level, whether the proportion exhibiting allergies is associated with the treatment.
Is the drug effective?
Explain your answer.

2 Of 120 onion seeds of variety A planted in an allotment 28 failed to germinate. Of 45 onion seeds of variety B planted in the allotment four failed to germinate. Form the data into a 2×2 contingency table and test whether the proportion failing to germinate is associated with the variety of seed.

3 Castings made from two different moulds were tested and the results are summarised in the following table:

	Mould 1	Mould 2
Satisfactory	88	165
Defective	12	15

Is the proportion defective independent of mould?

5

4 As part of a research study into pattern recognition, subjects were asked to examine a picture and see if they could distinguish a word. The picture contained the word 'technology' written backwards and camouflaged by an elaborate pattern. Of 23 librarians who took part 11 succeeded in recognising the word whilst of 19 designers, 13 succeeded. Form the data into a 2 × 2 contingency table and test at the 5% significance level, using Yates' continuity correction, whether an equal proportion of librarians and designers can distinguish the word. [A]

5 The data below refer to the 1996 general election in New Zealand. They show the winning party and the percentage turnout in a sample of constituencies.

Constituency	Winning party	Percentage turnout	Constituency	Winning party	Percentage turnout
Albany	National	87.42	Hunua	National	85.50
Aoraki	Labour	87.95	Hutt South	Labour	87.85
Auckland Central	Labour	88.08	Ham	National	89.22
Banks Peninsula	National	89.71	Kaikoura	National	86.56
Bay of Plenty	National	85.23	Karapiro	National	84.23
Christchurch Cent.	Labour	83.68	Mana	Labour	87.67
Christchurch East	Labour	86.10	Mangere	Labour	79.78
Clutha-Southland	National	84.75	Maungakiekie	National	85.28
Coromandel	National	86.47	Napier	Labour	86.95
Dunedin North	Labour	88.48	Nelson	National	86.88
Dunedin South	Labour	88.87	New Lynn	Labour	85.28
Epsom	National	89.15	North Shore	National	88.34
Hamilton East	National	86.89	Otaki	Labour	88.22
Hamilton West	National	85.09	Owairaka	Labour	86.74

(a) Classify the percentage turnout as 'less than 87' or 'greater than or equal to 87'. Hence draw up a 2 × 2 contingency table suitable for testing the hypothesis that the winning party is independent of the percentage turnout.

(b) Carry out the test using a 5% significance level.

(c) Identify a feature of the constituencies in the sample which suggests that they were not randomly selected. Discuss briefly whether this is likely to affect the validity of the test carried out in **(b)**. [A]

MIXED EXERCISE

1 A college office stocks statistical tables and various items of stationery for sale to students.
The number of items sold by the office and the percentage of these which were statistical tables are shown in the table below. The table gives figures for each of the first five weeks of the autumn term.

Week	1	2	3	4	5
Total number of items sold	216	200	166	105	64
% of items which were statistical tables	11	16	12	17	14

(The percentages have been rounded to the nearest whole number.)

   (a) Form the data above into a table suitable for testing whether the proportion of items which were statistical tables is independent of the week.

   (b) Carry out this test at the 5% significance level. [A]

2 A biology student observed snails on a bare limestone pavement and in a nearby woodland. The colour of each snail was classified as light or dark. The following table shows the number of snails observed in each category.

	Light	Dark
Pavement	17	10
Woodland	3	15

   (a) Use a χ^2 test at the 5% significance level to investigate whether there is an association between the colour of snails and their habitat.

   (b) Describe, briefly, the nature of the association, if any, between colour and habitat.

The biology teacher complained that, since fewer than five snails were observed in the Light/Woodland cell, the test carried out in (a) was not valid.

   (c) Comment on this complaint.

The weight, in grams, of a randomly selected snail in each category is recorded in the following table:

	Light	Dark
Pavement	14	12
Woodland	18	21

   (d) The geography teacher suggested that a χ^2 test should be applied to these data. Comment on this suggestion. [A]

3 As part of a social survey, one thousand randomly selected school leavers were sent a postal questionnaire in 1996. Completed questionnaires were returned by 712 school leavers. These 712 school leavers were asked to complete a further questionnaire in 1997. The table below shows their response to the 1997 questionnaire classified by their answers to a question on truancy in the 1996 survey.

	Persistent truant	Occasional truant	Never truant
Returned 1997 questionnaire	17	152	295
Failed to return 1997 questionnaire	23	104	121

(a) Use the χ^2 distribution, at the 5% significance level, to test whether returning the 1997 questionnaire is independent of the answer to the 1996 question on truancy.

(b) On the evidence available, state whether 1996 school leavers who played truant are more or less likely to return the 1997 questionnaire. Give a reason for your answer.

(c) A researcher estimated that the proportion of school leavers who played truant persistently in their last year at school was $\frac{40}{712}$.
Give two reasons why this might be an underestimate.

[A]

4 The following data are from *The British Medical Journal*. The table shows whether or not the subjects suffered from heart disease and how their snoring habits were classified by their partners.

	Never snores	Occasionally snores	Snores nearly every night	Snores every night
Heart disease	24	35	21	30
No heart disease	1355	603	192	224

(a) Use a χ^2 test, at the 5% significance level, to investigate whether frequency of snoring is related to heart disease.

(b) On the evidence above, do heart disease sufferers tend to snore more or snore less than others? Give a reason for your answer.

(c) Do these data show that snoring causes heart disease? Explain your answer briefly. [A]

5 An incurable illness, which is not life threatening, is usually treated with drugs to alleviate painful symptoms. A number of sufferers agreed to be placed at random into two groups. The members of one group would undergo a new treatment which involves major surgery and the members of the other group would continue with the standard drug treatment. Twelve months later a study of these sufferers produced information on their symptoms which is summarised in the following 2×4 contingency table:

	No change	Slight improvement	Marked improvement	Information unobtainable
New treatment	12	32	46	44
Standard treatment	36	39	12	33

(a) Test at the 5% significance level whether the outcome is independent of the treatment.

(b) Comment on the effectiveness of the new treatment in the light of your answer to **(a)**.

(c) Further analysis of the reasons for information being unobtainable from sufferers showed that of the 44 who underwent the new treatment 19 had died, 10 had refused to cooperate and the rest were untraceable. Of the 33 who continued with the standard treatment three had died, 12 had refused to cooperate and the rest were untraceable. Form these data into a 2×3 contingency table but do not carry out any further calculations. Given that for the contingency table you have formed $\Sigma \dfrac{(O - E)^2}{E} = 10.74$, test, at the 5% significance level, whether the reason for information being unobtainable is independent of the treatment.

(d) Comment on the effectiveness of the new treatment in the light of all the information in this question. [A]

Key point summary

1 A contingency table shows the frequencies of two (or more) variables simultaneously.   *p83*

2 The expected number in any cell of a contingency table is   *p84*

$$\frac{(\text{row total}) \times (\text{column total})}{(\text{grand total})}.$$

3 $X^2 = \Sigma \dfrac{(O - E)^2}{E}$ may be approximated by the   *p85*

χ² distribution provided:

(i) the *O*s are frequencies,

(ii) the *E*s are reasonably large, say >5.

4 An $m \times n$ contingency table has $(m - 1)(n - 1)$ *p85*
degrees of freedom.

5 If it is necessary to combine classes to increase the   *p93*
size of the *E*s the most similar classes should be
combined.

6 For a 2 ×2 table, $\Sigma \dfrac{(|O - E| - 0.5)^2}{E}$ should be   *p98*

calculated. This is known as Yates' correction.

Test yourself	What to review
1 How many degrees of freedom has a 4 × 3 contingency table?	*Section 5.1*
2 When is Yates' correction applied?	*Section 5.3*
3 Find the appropriate critical value for analysing a 5 × 4 contingency table, using a 1% significance level.	*Section 5.1*
4 Why are two-sided tests not generally used when analysing contingency tables?	*Section 5.1*
5 A 2 × 4 contingency contains one cell with an expected value less than five. Why is it incorrect to combine this cell with a neighbouring cell and calculate $X^2 = \Sigma \dfrac{(O - E)^2}{E}$ for the resulting seven cells?	*Section 5.2*
6 Forty males and 50 females choose their favourite colour. A total of 24 choose red. If the results are tabulated in a contingency table, find the expected value for the female/red cell.	*Section 5.1*

Test yourself ANSWERS

1 6.

2 When a 2 × 2 contingency table is analysed.

3 26.2.

4 A low value of $\Sigma \dfrac{(O - E)^2}{E}$ indicates very good agreement between observed and expected values and hence is not a reason for rejecting the null hypothesis.

5 The resulting seven cells would no longer form a contingency table.

6 13.3.

Exam style practice paper

Time allowed 1 hour 45 minutes

Answer **all** questions

---

1 Travellers (excluding season ticket holders) on a city centre tram must purchase tickets from a machine on the platform which only accepts coins. The cost, £X, of a ticket depends on the destination of the journey and may be modelled by the following probability distribution.

x	$P(X = x)$
0.8	0.26
1.2	0.34
1.6	0.18
2.0	0.10
2.8	0.12

  (a) Calculate the mean and standard deviation of X.   (*6 marks*)

  (b) A visitor to the city who is not aware of the need to pay with coins arrives on the platform carrying £1.44 in change. Find the probability the visitor is able to buy an appropriate ticket. Assume that the distribution adequately models the cost of the ticket required by the visitor.   (*1 mark*)

  (c) Explain why the answer to **(b)** might not apply to a regular (non-season ticket holder) user of the tram who is carrying £1.44 in change.   (*2 marks*)

2 Applicants for an assembly job take a test of manual dexterity. Current employees took an average of 60 s to complete the test. The times, in seconds, taken to complete the test by a random sample of applicants were,

      63   125   77   49   74   67   59   66   102

(a) Stating clearly your null and alternative hypotheses, investigate, at the 5% significance level, whether the mean time taken by applicants to complete the test is greater than that taken by current employees. *(11 marks)*

(b) It later emerged that due to a misunderstanding of how the test should be timed all the recorded times for the new applicants were five seconds too long. Does this further information affect your conclusion in (a)? *(4 marks)*

3 A random sample of adults from three different areas of a city was asked whether they would prefer more money to be spent on public services or a reduction in the tax on petrol. The replies are summarised in the following table:

	Area		
	A	**B**	**C**
More money on public services	24	32	44
Reduce petrol tax	76	38	36

(a) Investigate at the 5% significance level whether the answer to the question is independent of the area. *(12 marks)*

The data is separated into two 3×2 contingency tables. The first containing the responses from the members of the sample who had access to private cars for their personal use and the second containing the responses from members of the sample who did not have access to private cars for their personal use. A statistician calculated the value of $\sum \dfrac{(O - E)^2}{E}$ to be 2.99 for the first table and 4.27 for the second table.

(b) Investigate at the 5% significance level whether the answer to the question is independent of area for those who have:

(i) access to a private car for their personal use,

(ii) no access to a private car for their personal use. *(2 marks)*

(c) Interpret your results. *(3 marks)*

4 In order to reduce the cost of telephone calls a family fits a device to their telephone which automatically cuts off each outgoing call after five minutes. Following this the length, in minutes, of calls made can be modelled by a random variable, X, with probability density function

$$f(x) = \begin{cases} kx^2 & 0 < x < 5 \\ 0 & \text{elsewhere} \end{cases}$$

(a) Verify that $k = 0.024$. *(3 marks)*

(b) Find the mean and standard deviation of X. *(9 marks)*

(c) Previously the average length of calls was five minutes. If calls cost 3p per minute and the family makes an average of 48 calls per week, find the average weekly savings. *(3 marks)*

5 A 'safer routes to school' campaign is to be undertaken by a city council which wishes to encourage parents and children to walk or cycle to school rather than to use private cars. As a first step it is decided to estimate the mean distance travelled to school by junior school children.

In a pilot study the following distances, in miles, travelled by a sample of children in the city were obtained:

    1.2   0.1   0.7   0.8   0.2   0.1   3.9   0.3   0.1   1.1

(a) Calculate a 95% confidence interval for the mean distance travelled to school by all junior school children in the city. *(8 marks)*

(b) State two assumptions you needed to make in order to answer **(a)**. *(2 marks)*

(c) Does the data provide any reason to suspect that one necessary assumption may not be true? Explain your answer. *(2 marks)*

In a larger survey, a random sample of 140 junior school children in the city were found to travel a mean distance of 1.01 miles with a standard deviation of 0.98 miles.

(d) Calculate a 90% confidence interval for the mean distance travelled to school by junior school children in the city. *(4 marks)*

(e) Explain why you did not need to make any assumptions to calculate the confidence interval in **(d)**. *(3 marks)*

(f) Find, approximately, the size of sample necessary to obtain an 80% confidence interval of width 0.1 miles for the mean distance travelled by junior school children in the city. *(5 marks)*

Appendix

Table 3 Normal distribution function

The table gives the probability p that a normally distributed random variable Z, with mean = 0 and variance = 1, is less than or equal to z.

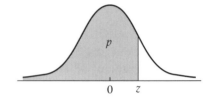

z	0.00	0.01	0.02	0.03	0.04	0.05	0.06	0.07	0.08	0.09	z
0.0	0.50000	0.50399	0.50798	0.51197	0.51595	0.51994	0.52392	0.52790	0.53188	0.53586	0.0
0.1	0.53983	0.54380	0.54776	0.55172	0.55567	0.55962	0.56356	0.56749	0.57142	0.57535	0.1
0.2	0.57926	0.58317	0.58706	0.59095	0.59483	0.59871	0.60257	0.60642	0.61026	0.61409	0.2
0.3	0.61791	0.62172	0.62552	0.62930	0.63307	0.63683	0.64058	0.64431	0.64803	0.65173	0.3
0.4	0.65542	0.65910	0.66276	0.66640	0.67003	0.67364	0.67724	0.68082	0.68439	0.68793	0.4
0.5	0.69146	0.69497	0.69847	0.70194	0.70540	0.70884	0.71226	0.71566	0.71904	0.72240	0.5
0.6	0.72575	0.72907	0.73237	0.73565	0.73891	0.74215	0.74537	0.74857	0.75175	0.75490	0.6
0.7	0.75804	0.76115	0.76424	0.76730	0.77035	0.77337	0.77637	0.77935	0.78230	0.78524	0.7
0.8	0.78814	0.79103	0.79389	0.79673	0.79955	0.80234	0.80511	0.80785	0.81057	0.81327	0.8
0.9	0.81594	0.81859	0.82121	0.82381	0.82639	0.82894	0.83147	0.83398	0.83646	0.83891	0.9
1.0	0.84134	0.84375	0.84614	0.84849	0.85083	0.85314	0.85543	0.85769	0.85993	0.86214	1.0
1.1	0.86433	0.86650	0.86864	0.87076	0.87286	0.87493	0.87698	0.87900	0.88100	0.88298	1.1
1.2	0.88493	0.88686	0.88877	0.89065	0.89251	0.89435	0.89617	0.89796	0.89973	0.90147	1.2
1.3	0.90320	0.90490	0.90658	0.90824	0.90988	0.91149	0.91309	0.91466	0.91621	0.91774	1.3
1.4	0.91924	0.92073	0.92220	0.92364	0.92507	0.92647	0.92785	0.92922	0.93056	0.93189	1.4
1.5	0.93319	0.93448	0.93574	0.93699	0.93822	0.93943	0.94062	0.94179	0.94295	0.94408	1.5
1.6	0.94520	0.94630	0.94738	0.94845	0.94950	0.95053	0.95154	0.95254	0.95352	0.95449	1.6
1.7	0.95543	0.95637	0.95728	0.95818	0.95907	0.95994	0.96080	0.96164	0.96246	0.96327	1.7
1.8	0.96407	0.96485	0.96562	0.96638	0.96712	0.96784	0.96856	0.96926	0.96995	0.97062	1.8
1.9	0.97128	0.97193	0.97257	0.97320	0.97381	0.97441	0.97500	0.97558	0.97615	0.97670	1.9
2.0	0.97725	0.97778	0.97831	0.97882	0.97932	0.97982	0.98030	0.98077	0.98124	0.98169	2.0
2.1	0.98214	0.98257	0.98300	0.98341	0.98382	0.98422	0.98461	0.98500	0.98537	0.98574	2.1
2.2	0.98610	0.98645	0.98679	0.98679	0.98713	0.98745	0.98778	0.98809	0.98840	0.98899	2.2
2.3	0.98928	0.98956	0.98983	0.99010	0.99036	0.99061	0.99086	0.99111	0.99134	0.99158	2.3
2.4	0.99180	0.99202	0.99224	0.99245	0.99266	0.99286	0.99305	0.99324	0.99343	0.99361	2.4
2.5	0.99379	0.99396	0.99413	0.99430	0.99446	0.99461	0.99477	0.99492	0.99506	0.99520	2.5
2.6	0.99534	0.99547	0.99560	0.99573	0.99585	0.99598	0.99609	0.99621	0.99632	0.99643	2.6
2.7	0.99653	0.99664	0.99674	0.99683	0.99693	0.99702	0.99711	0.99720	0.99728	0.99736	2.7
2.8	0.99744	0.99752	0.99760	0.99767	0.99774	0.99781	0.99788	0.99795	0.99801	0.99807	2.8
2.9	0.99813	0.99819	0.99825	0.99831	0.99836	0.99841	0.99846	0.99851	0.99856	0.99861	2.9
3.0	0.99865	0.99869	0.99874	0.99878	0.99882	0.99886	0.99889	0.99893	0.99896	0.99900	3.0
3.1	0.99903	0.99906	0.99910	0.99913	0.99916	0.99918	0.99921	0.99924	0.99926	0.99929	3.1
3.2	0.99931	0.99934	0.99936	0.99938	0.99940	0.99942	0.99944	0.99946	0.99948	0.99950	3.2
3.3	0.99952	0.99953	0.99955	0.99957	0.99958	0.99960	0.99961	0.99962	0.99964	0.99965	3.3
3.4	0.99966	0.99968	0.99969	0.99970	0.99971	0.99972	0.99973	0.99974	0.99975	0.99976	3.4
3.5	0.99977	0.99978	0.99978	0.99979	0.99980	0.99981	0.99981	0.99982	0.99983	0.99983	3.5
3.6	0.99984	0.99985	0.99985	0.99986	0.99986	0.99987	0.99987	0.99988	0.99988	0.99989	3.6
3.7	0.99989	0.99990	0.99990	0.99990	0.99991	0.99991	0.99992	0.99992	0.99992	0.99992	3.7
3.8	0.99993	0.99993	0.99993	0.99994	0.99994	0.99994	0.99994	0.99995	0.99995	0.99995	3.8
3.9	0.99995	0.99995	0.99996	0.99996	0.99996	0.99996	0.99996	0.99996	0.99997	0.99997	3.9

Table 4 Percentage points of the normal distribution

The table gives the values of z satisfying $P(Z \leq z) = p$, where Z is the normally distributed random variable with mean $= 0$ and variance $= 1$.

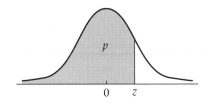

p	0.00	0.01	0.02	0.03	0.04	0.05	0.06	0.07	0.08	0.09	p
0.5	0.0000	0.0251	0.0502	0.0753	0.1004	0.1257	0.1510	0.1764	0.2019	0.2275	0.5
0.6	0.2533	0.2793	0.3055	0.3319	0.3585	0.3853	0.4125	0.4399	0.4677	0.4958	0.6
0.7	0.5244	0.5534	0.5828	0.6128	0.6433	0.6745	0.7063	0.7388	0.7722	0.8064	0.7
0.8	0.8416	0.8779	0.9154	0.9542	0.9945	1.0364	1.0803	1.1264	1.1750	1.2265	0.8
0.9	1.2816	1.3408	1.4051	1.4758	1.5548	1.6449	1.7507	1.8808	2.0537	2.3263	0.9

p	0.000	0.001	0.002	0.003	0.004	0.005	0.006	0.007	0.008	0.009	p
0.95	1.6449	1.6546	1.6646	1.6747	1.6849	1.6954	1.7060	1.7169	1.7279	1.7392	0.95
0.96	1.7507	1.7624	1.7744	1.7866	1.7991	1.8119	1.8250	1.8384	1.8522	1.8663	0.96
0.97	1.8808	1.8957	1.9110	1.9268	1.9431	1.9600	1.9774	1.9954	2.0141	2.0335	0.97
0.98	2.0537	2.0749	2.0969	2.1201	2.1444	2.1701	2.1973	2.2262	2.2571	2.2904	0.98
0.99	2.3263	2.3656	2.4089	2.4573	2.5121	2.5758	2.6521	2.7478	2.8782	3.0902	0.99

Table 5 Percentage points of the student's t distribution

The table gives the values of x satisfying $P(X \leqslant x) = p$, where X is a random variable having the Student's t distribution with ν degrees of freedom.

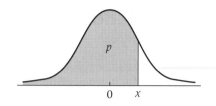

ν \ p	0.9	0.95	0.975	0.99	0.995
1	3.078	6.314	12.706	31.821	63.657
2	1.886	2.920	4.303	6.965	9.925
3	1.638	2.353	3.182	4.541	5.841
4	1.533	2.132	2.776	3.747	4.604
5	1.476	2.015	2.571	3.365	4.032
6	1.440	1.943	2.447	3.143	3.707
7	1.415	1.895	2.365	2.998	3.499
8	1.397	1.860	2.306	2.896	3.355
9	1.383	1.833	2.262	2.821	3.250
10	1.372	1.812	2.228	2.764	3.169
11	1.363	1.796	2.201	2.718	3.106
12	1.356	1.782	2.179	2.681	3.055
13	1.350	1.771	2.160	2.650	3.012
14	1.345	1.761	2.145	2.624	2.977
15	1.341	1.753	2.131	2.602	2.947
16	1.337	1.746	2.121	2.583	2.921
17	1.333	1.740	2.110	2.567	2.898
18	1.330	1.734	2.101	2.552	2.878
19	1.328	1.729	2.093	2.539	2.861
20	1.325	1.725	2.086	2.528	2.845
21	1.323	1.721	2.080	2.518	2.831
22	1.321	1.717	2.074	2.508	2.819
23	1.319	1.714	2.069	2.500	2.807
24	1.318	1.711	2.064	2.492	2.797
25	1.316	1.708	2.060	2.485	2.787
26	1.315	1.706	2.056	2.479	2.779
27	1.314	1.703	2.052	2.473	2.771
28	1.313	1.701	2.048	2.467	2.763

ν \ p	0.9	0.95	0.975	0.99	0.995
29	1.311	1.699	2.045	2.462	2.756
30	1.310	1.697	2.042	2.457	2.750
31	1.309	1.696	2.040	2.453	2.744
32	1.309	1.694	2.037	2.449	2.738
33	1.308	1.692	2.035	2.445	2.733
34	1.307	1.691	2.032	2.441	2.728
35	1.306	1.690	2.030	2.438	2.724
36	1.306	1.688	2.028	2.434	2.719
37	1.305	1.687	2.026	2.431	2.715
38	1.304	1.686	2.024	2.429	2.712
39	1.304	1.685	2.023	2.426	2.708
40	1.303	1.684	2.021	2.423	2.704
45	1.301	1.679	2.014	2.412	2.690
50	1.299	1.676	2.009	2.403	2.678
55	1.297	1.673	2.004	2.396	2.668
60	1.296	1.671	2.000	2.390	2.660
65	1.295	1.669	1.997	2.385	2.654
70	1.294	1.667	1.994	2.381	2.648
75	1.293	1.665	1.992	2.377	2.643
80	1.292	1.664	1.990	2.374	2.639
85	1.292	1.663	1.998	2.371	2.635
90	1.291	1.662	1.987	2.368	2.632
95	1.291	1.661	1.985	2.366	2.629
100	1.290	1.660	1.984	2.364	2.626
125	1.288	1.657	1.979	2.357	2.616
150	1.287	1.655	1.976	2.351	2.609
200	1.286	1.653	1.972	2.345	2.601
∞	1.282	1.645	1.960	2.326	2.576

Table 6 Percentage points of the χ^2 distribution

The table gives the values of x satisfying $P(X \leqslant X) = p$, where X is a random variable having the χ^2 distribution with ν degrees of freedom.

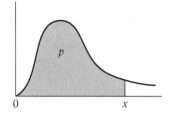

ν \ p	0.005	0.01	0.025	0.05	0.1	0.9	0.95	0.975	0.99	0.995	p \ ν
1	0.00004	0.0002	0.001	0.004	0.016	2.706	3.841	5.024	6.635	7.879	1
2	0.010	0.020	0.051	0.103	0.211	4.605	5.991	7.378	9.210	10.597	2
3	0.072	0.115	0.216	0.352	0.584	6.251	7.815	9.348	11.345	12.838	3
4	0.207	0.297	0.484	0.711	1.064	7.779	9.488	11.143	13.277	14.860	4
5	0.412	0.554	0.831	1.145	1.610	9.236	11.070	12.833	15.086	16.750	5
6	0.676	0.872	1.237	1.635	2.204	10.645	12.592	14.449	16.812	18.548	6
7	0.989	1.239	1.690	2.167	2.833	12.017	14.067	16.013	18.475	20.278	7
8	1.344	1.646	2.180	2.733	3.490	13.362	15.507	17.535	20.090	21.955	8
9	1.735	2.088	2.700	3.325	4.168	14.684	16.919	19.023	21.666	23.589	9
10	2.156	2.558	3.247	3.940	4.865	15.987	18.307	20.483	23.209	25.188	10
11	2.603	3.053	3.816	4.575	5.578	17.275	19.675	21.920	24.725	26.757	11
12	3.074	3.571	4.404	5.226	6.304	18.549	21.026	23.337	26.217	28.300	12
13	3.565	4.107	5.009	5.892	7.042	19.812	22.362	24.736	27.688	29.819	13
14	4.075	4.660	5.629	6.571	7.790	21.064	23.685	26.119	29.141	31.319	14
15	4.601	5.229	6.262	7.261	8.547	22.307	24.996	27.488	30.578	32.801	15
16	5.142	5.812	6.908	7.962	9.312	23.542	26.296	28.845	32.000	34.267	16
17	5.697	6.408	7.564	8.672	10.085	24.769	27.587	30.191	33.409	35.718	17
18	6.265	7.015	8.231	9.390	10.865	25.989	28.869	31.526	34.805	37.156	18
19	6.844	7.633	8.907	10.117	11.651	27.204	30.144	32.852	36.191	38.582	19
20	7.434	8.260	9.591	10.851	12.443	28.412	31.410	34.170	37.566	39.997	20
21	8.034	8.897	10.283	11.591	13.240	29.615	32.671	35.479	38.932	41.401	21
22	8.643	9.542	10.982	12.338	14.041	30.813	33.924	36.781	40.289	42.796	22
23	9.260	10.196	11.689	13.091	14.848	32.007	35.172	38.076	41.638	44.181	23
24	9.886	10.856	12.401	13.848	15.659	33.196	36.415	39.364	42.980	45.559	24
25	10.520	11.524	13.120	14.611	16.473	34.382	37.652	40.646	44.314	46.928	25
26	11.160	12.198	13.844	15.379	17.292	35.563	38.885	41.923	45.642	48.290	26
27	11.808	12.879	14.573	16.151	18.114	36.741	40.113	43.195	46.963	49.645	27
28	12.461	13.565	15.308	16.928	18.939	37.916	41.337	44.461	48.278	50.993	28
29	13.121	14.256	16.047	17.708	19.768	39.087	42.557	45.722	49.588	52.336	29
30	13.787	14.953	16.791	18.493	20.599	40.256	43.773	46.979	50.892	53.672	30
31	14.458	15.655	17.539	19.281	21.434	41.422	44.985	48.232	52.191	55.003	31
32	15.134	16.362	18.291	20.072	22.271	42.585	46.194	49.480	53.486	56.328	32
33	15.815	17.074	19.047	20.867	23.110	43.745	47.400	50.725	54.776	57.648	33
34	16.501	17.789	19.806	21.664	23.952	44.903	48.602	51.996	56.061	58.964	34
35	17.192	18.509	20.569	22.465	24.797	46.059	49.802	53.203	57.342	60.275	35
36	17.887	19.223	21.336	23.269	25.643	47.212	50.998	54.437	58.619	61.581	36
37	18.586	19.960	22.106	24.075	26.492	48.363	52.192	55.668	59.892	62.883	37
38	19.289	20.691	22.878	24.884	27.343	49.513	53.384	56.896	61.162	64.181	38
39	19.996	21.426	23.654	25.695	28.196	50.660	54.572	58.120	62.428	65.476	39
40	20.707	22.164	24.433	26.509	29.051	51.805	55.758	59.342	63.691	66.766	40
45	24.311	25.901	28.366	30.612	33.350	57.505	61.656	65.410	69.957	73.166	45
50	27.991	29.707	32.357	34.764	37.689	63.167	67.505	71.420	76.154	79.490	50
55	31.735	33.570	36.398	38.958	42.060	68.796	73.311	77.380	82.292	85.749	55
60	35.534	37.485	40.482	43.188	46.459	74.397	79.082	83.298	88.379	91.952	60
65	39.383	41.444	44.603	47.450	50.883	79.973	84.821	89.177	94.422	98.105	65
70	43.275	45.442	48.758	51.739	55.329	85.527	90.531	95.023	100.425	104.215	70
75	47.206	49.475	52.942	56.054	59.795	91.061	96.217	100.839	106.393	110.286	75
80	51.172	53.540	57.153	60.391	64.278	96.578	101.879	106.629	112.329	116.321	80
85	55.170	57.634	61.389	64.749	68.777	102.079	107.522	112.393	118.236	122.325	85
90	59.196	61.754	65.647	69.126	73.291	107.565	113.145	118.136	124.116	128.299	90
95	63.250	65.898	69.925	73.520	77.818	113.038	118.752	123.858	129.973	134.247	95
100	67.328	70.065	74.222	77.929	82.358	118.498	124.342	129.561	135.807	140.169	100

Answers

EXERCISE 1A

1 1, 1, 1.

2 2.3, 8.41, 2.9.

3 (a) 0.1;   **(b)** 1.5, 1.45, 1.20.

4 2, 1.41.

5 (a) 1.7, 1.18;   **(b)** 4.76.

6 (a) 4, 2.83;   **(b)**

x	0	5
$P(X = x)$	0.5	0.5

7 (a) 68.8, 21.6;   **(b)** 0.0464.

8 (a) 1.34, 1.83;   **(b) (i)** binomial,   **(ii)** 1.25, 0.968;

   (c) Means fairly similar, standard deviations very different. Suggests applicants not guessing and their distribution not binomial.

9 (a) 3.62, 1.95;   **(b)** 1.82 + 3.5p, increase in sales if p > 0.514.

EXERCISE 1B

1 (a) $\frac{2}{3}$;   **(b)** 1.56, 0.0802, 0.283.

2 2.5, 1.12.

3 (a) 1.5, 0.387;   **(b)** 0.422.

4 (a) 1.4, 0.447;   **(b)** 0.2.

5 0.833, 0.589.

6 (b) 1.33, 0.943;   **(c)** 0.387.

7 (a) 0.125;   **(b)** 0.4375 > 0.3085;

   (c) Q (10.7);   **(d)** P − 40p Q − 38.3p − P higher.

EXERCISE 1C

1 (a) 0.2;   **(b)** 6.5, 2.08;   **(c)** 1.44.

2 (a) 0.1;   **(b)** 0;   **(c)** 0.3;   **(d)** 5, 2.89.

3 (a) 0.2;   **(b)** 0;   **(c)** 0.2;   **(d)** 1.5, 2.08, 1.44.

4 (a) 12.5;   **(b)** 0, 0.0231;   **(c)** 0.5;   **(d)** 0.125.

5 (a) 0.7;   **(b)** 0.6;   **(c)** 0.7.

MIXED EXERCISE

1 (a) $\dfrac{a}{2}, \dfrac{a}{\sqrt{12}};$ (b) $\dfrac{a}{2}, \dfrac{a}{\sqrt{12n}};$ (c) $\dfrac{a}{2}, \dfrac{a^2}{20}.$

2 (a) 1.19, 1.06;   (b) (i) Poisson,   (ii) 1.09;

  (c) Standard deviations similar so Poisson plausible, suggesting cars passing at random at a constant average rate.

3 (a) (ii) 2.67, 0.943,   (iii) 0.4375;

  (b) (i)

0–1	0.0625	6
1–2	0.1875	10
2–3	0.3125	14
3–4	0.4375	18

    (ii) 14.5, 3.71.

4 (a) $a = 0.02,$ $c = \frac{1}{15};$

  (b) (i) 6.67,   (ii) 3.67,   (iii) 51.8;   (c) 0.45.

5 (a) 0.25, 0.0817;   (c) 1.2;   (d) 0.0307;

  (e) 0.00920;   (f) 0.211.

2 Confidence intervals

EXERCISE 2A

1 (a) 58.64–60.00;   (b) 58.81–59.83;   (c) 59.10–59.54.

2 (a) (i) 65.0–82.2, (ii) 63.3–83.8,   (iii) 60.1–87.0;

  (b) (i) 83.9–97.3, (ii) 80.4–100.8,   (iii) 77.1–104.1;

  (c) Athletes seem to have a lower mean diastolic blood pressure than for the population of healthy adults (84.8 is above the 95% confidence interval, although it is just inside the 99% interval). On this evidence chess club members are consistent with the population of healthy adults as 84.8 lies within the confidence intervals.

3 63.5–115.5.

4 (a) 101.7–159.2;   (b) 29.3–174.1;

  (c) Station manager's claim is incorrect. Even making the lowest reasonable estimate of the mean the great majority of passengers will queue for more than 25 s.

5 (a) 494.69–499.63;   (b) (i) 7.5 g,   (ii) 440.3–478.9;

  (c) Confidence interval calculated in (a) suggests that the mean weight of pickles in a jar is above 454 g but interval calculated in (b) suggests that many individual jars will contain less than 454 g of pickles.

EXERCISE 2B

1 93.6–101.4.

2 (a) 812.2–883.8;   (b) 831.3–864.7.

3 (a) 72.54–75.46;

  (b) No difficulty as sample is large so mean will be approximately normally distributed.

4 (a) (i) 2.717–2.755, **(ii)** 2.679–2.701; **(b)** 2.608–2.772;

(c) Confidence intervals do not overlap so mean for soft centres clearly greater than mean for hard centres. However interval calculated in **(b)** shows that many hard centred chocolates are bigger than the mean of the soft centred chocolates. Diameter not a great deal of use because of large amount of overlap.

5 (a) 201.35–208.51; **(b) (i)** 0.150, **(ii)** 0.0265;

(c) Average weight okay, too large a proportion less than 191 g and less than 182 g. This could be rectified by increasing the mean. Meeting the requirements in this way will mean that the mean contents are quite a lot over the nominal weight. Reducing the standard deviation is expensive but would allow the requirements to be met with a small reduction in the current mean contents.

EXERCISE 2C

1 (a) 266–516; **(b)** 0.1.

2 (a) (i) 2640–3080, **(ii)** 139;

(b) (i) Some uncertainty as sample is small,

(ii) No problem as sample is large;

(c) Some doubt as if standard deviation is 300, the sample range is only about 1.5 standard deviations (or estimated standard deviation only 184).

3 (b) 0.667, 0.471;

(c) 0.777–1.023. Since sample is large the sample mean can be assumed to be approximately normally distributed even though X is clearly not normally distributed.

4 (a) (i) 193.1–200.1, **(ii)** 195.1–198.1;

(b) (i) 0.05, **(ii)** 0.05; **(c)** 0.02.

5 (a) 925–1092;

(b) No substantial evidence of any difference;

(c) 167; **(d)** 75.8; **(e)** 20.

6 (a) (ii) 2.67, 0.943; **(b)** 3.66–3.94;

(c) Assumed the 120 calls could be treated as a random sample of Debbie's calls;

(d) 2.67 far below confidence interval calculated. Model appears to be unsatisfactory.

EXERCISE 2D

1 (a) 93.50–98.50;

(b) Operating time reduced – overhaul effective.

2 (a) 220.69–224.65; **(c)** 219.47–225.86;

(b) 220.06–225.28; **(d)** 218.15–227.18.

3 (a) (i) 2347.5–2399.4, **(ii)** 2329.6–2417.2;

(b) First confidence interval uses data from past experience. Likely to be more accurate unless standard deviation has changed. Second confidence is valid whether or not standard deviation is 35.

4 (a) (i)   510.09–514.25,   **(ii)** 508.69–515.64;

  (b) First confidence interval uses data from past experience. Likely to be more accurate unless standard deviation has changed. Second confidence is valid whether or not standard deviation is 2.6.

5 (a) 24.52–29.64;   **(b)** 18.85;

  (c) 7.40   Regulations appear to be adequate as 7.40 is well below the load at which an anchor might fail.

6 (a) 18.9–63.1;

  (b) Sample random and population normally distributed;

  (c) 32.5–40.1;

  (d) Still need to assume sample random. Normal distribution not necessary as sample large.

3 Hypothesis testing

EXERCISE 3A

1 ts 1.80   cv 1.6449   mean greater than 135 kg.

2 ts −1.22   cv ±1.96   accept mean reaction time 7.5 s.

3 ts 1.05   cv 1.6449   accept children don't take longer.

4 ts −3.48   cv ±2.5758   mean length not satisfactory.

5 ts 1.67   cv 1.6449   silver not pure.

6 ts 3.19   cv 2.3263   mean weight has increased.

7 ts −1.57   cv −1.6449   mean weight not reduced.

8 ts 3.95   cv ±1.96   mean time greater than 4 s.

EXERCISE 3B

1 (a) (i)   Conclude mean greater than 135 kg when in fact mean equals 135 kg,

  (ii) Conclude mean equals 135 kg when in fact mean greater than 135 kg;

  (b) (i) 0.05,   **(ii)** 0.

2 (a) (i)   Conclude mean unsatisfactory when it is satisfactory,

  (ii) Conclude mean is satisfactory when it is unsatisfactory;

  (b) (i) 0.01,   **(ii)** 0.

3 (a) ts −1.80   cv ±1.96   accept mean time is 20 minutes;

  (b) Conclude mean time not 20min when in fact it is 20 minutes;

  (c) would need to know the actual value of the mean.

4 (a) ts −1.69   cv ±1.6449   mean length less than 19.25 mm;

  (b) (i) Conclude mean not 19.25 mm when in fact it is 19.25 mm,

  (ii) Conclude mean 19.25 mm when in fact it is not 19.25 mm;

  (c) 0.1.

5 (a) ts −1.90   cv −1.6449   easier to assemble;

(b) Conclude not easier to assemble when in fact it is.

4 Further hypothesis testing for means

EXERCISE 4A

1 ts 2.42   cv 2.3263   mean breaking strength greater than 195 kg.

2 ts 1.02   cv ±1.96   mean resistance 1.5 Ω.

3 ts −2.67   cv −1.6449   mean test score lower.

4 ts 1.79   cv 1.6449   mean weight greater than 500 g.

5 ts −2.19   cv −2.3263   suspicions not correct.

Sample assumed random.

6 ts 1.87   cv 2.3263   mean weight not greater than 35 g.

7 (a) ts −4.98   cv −1.6449   mean less than 7.4;

(b) Test statistic is −4.98 so conclusion would have been unchanged even if the significance level had been very much less than 5%. Conclusion is very clear;

(c) As the sample is large it is not necessary to make any assumption about the distribution. However it is necessary to assume the sample is random. There is no information on this. If, for example, only those with particular symptoms had been tested they might be untypical of all varicoceles sufferers.

EXERCISE 4B

1 ts -0.532   cv ±2.179   mean length 50 cm.

2 ts 1.43   cv 1.363   mean exceeds 25 kg.

3 ts 2.78   cv 1.771   mean greater than 120 kg.

4 ts −0.937   cv −1.761   mean time not less than 2 minutes.

5 ts −2.36   cv ±2.228   mean less than 95

assumed distribution normal.

6 ts −2.45   cv −2.896   new mean not smaller.

MIXED EXERCISE

1 ts −2.27 (assuming $\sigma = 0.25$)   cv ±1.96 readings biased.

2 (a) ts −1.35   cv ±1.734   mean diameter 275 mm;

(b) Use $\sigma = 5$, ts −1.74, cv ±1.6449 from normal tables, conclude mean diameter less than 275 mm.

3 ts 12.4   cv ±2.5758   mean dust deposit greater than 60 g.

4 ts −2.11   cv −1.6449   mean score for new ice cream lower.

5 ts 1.48   cv ±1.812   mean mark 40.

6 ts 2.14   cv 1.6449   mean higher than 77.4 mm.

7 (a) ts 1.49   cv ±2.365   mean 40 minutes;

(b) Time of three hours was due to exceptional circumstances. If manager wants to examine mean time under normal circumstances it is appropriate to exclude this one. If manager wishes to examine mean time under all circumstances the time of three hours should be considered. If it is included the assumption of normal distribution will be violated.

8 (a) ts 1.91   cv 1.6449   mean life longer;

(b) use value estimated from sample for standard deviation and obtain critical value from t distribution;

(c) ts 1.30   cv 1.833   mean life not longer.
This conclusion does not mean that we have proved the mean is 960 days only that there is insufficient evidence to disprove it. With the additional information that the standard deviation was 135 days there was sufficient evidence to show that the mean was more than 960 days subject to a risk of 5% of claiming an increase when no increase exists.

9 (a) ts 3.19   cv ±1.96   mean take home pay greater than £140;

(b) (i) large sample so conclusions not affected (central limit theorem),

(ii) conclusion unreliable – for example, whole sample could have been taken from one employer who paid relatively high wages.

10 (a) ts 1.54   cv 1.6449   mean mark not higher;

(b) mean of large sample approximately normally distributed by central limit theorem;

(c) sample was self selected. Probably children of highly motivated/gullible parents. Conclusion unreliable since sample not random.

5 Contingency tables

EXERCISE 5A

1 $X^2 = 38.7$ cv 9.21   time of day associated with type of birth.

2 $X^2 = 23.8$ cv 9.21   proportion favouring road improvements not independent of area.

3 $X^2 = 6.66$ cv 7.815   accept choice of dish independent of day of week.

4 (a) Only women in the main shopping area asked (many other answers possible);

(b) $X^2 = 17.7$ cv 9.49   respondents' replies not independent of age.

5 (a) $X^2 = 17.0$ cv 5.99   proportion transferred not independent of surgeon;

(b) B had substantially less transferred than expected. Need to know how cases were allocated. It could be, say, that only straightforward operations were undertaken by B.

6 (a) $X^2 = 11.4$ cv 9.21   sex and grade not independent;

(b) Females did better - more than expected obtained high grades and less than expected had low grades;

(c) (i) Need total number of candidates in order to calculate frequencies,

   (ii) cv 10.6   subject and grade not independent,

   (iii) A bigger proportion of statistics candidates than pure and applied candidates obtained high grades. Would need some information on quality and preparation of candidates to say whether it is easier to get a good grade in statistics.

7 $X^2 = 16.9$ cv 13.3

Grade and length of employment not independent. Unskilled staff tend to stay longer than skilled staff. In particular more unskilled employees than expected stay longer than five years and more skilled staff than expected leave within two years.

EXERCISE 5B

1 $X^2 = 12.4$ cv 5.99   age and sex not independent.

2 $X^2 = 3.14$ cv 7.815   (5%) (another % could be chosen as not specified in question) accept choice independent of gender.

3 $X^2 = 1.99$ cv 9.21   accept method of communication independent of subject.

4 (a) $X^2 = 35.3$ cv 7.815   proportion of guests rating a feature important not independent of feature;

(b) Availability of squash courts much less important than other features. Little to choose between other features – number rating them important exceeded expected number by roughly the same proportion;

(c) If $E < 5$;

(d) Comfortable beds – most similar category;

(e) cv between 73.3 and 79.1. Rating and feature not independent.

EXERCISE 5C

1 $X^2 = 5.73$ cv 3.84   proportion exhibiting allergies not independent of treatment. Drug effective – less than expected of those receiving the drug exhibited allergies.

2 $X^2 = 3.50$ cv 3.84   (5%) (another % could be used) accept proportion germinating independent of variety.

3 $X^2 = 0.618$ cv 3.84   accept proportion defective independent of mould.

4 $X^2 = 1.06$ cv 3.84   accept equal proportion of librarians and designers can distinguish the word.

5 (a)

	<87%	>87%
National	10	5
Labour	6	7

(b) $X^2 = 0.507$ cv 3.84   accept winning party independent of turnout;

(c) Constituencies appear to have been selected in alphabetical order. No constituencies from last part of alphabet. This could effect the test but election results unlikely to be associated with name of constituency so test probably valid. (Other answers possible.)

MIXED EXERCISE

1 (a)

Week	1	2	3	4	5
Statistics tables	24	32	20	18	9
Other items	192	168	146	87	55

(b) $X^2 = 3.56$ cv 9.49 accept proportion of items which were statistical tables independent of week.

2 (a) $X^2 = 7.59$ cv 3.84 colour not independent of habitat;

(b) Greater proportion of woodland snails dark;

(c) Test valid since $Es > 5$;

(d) Test not valid since Os are not frequencies.

3 (a) $X^2 = 18.9$ cv 5.99 returning 1997 questionnaire not independent of answer to 1996 question on truancy;

(b) Less likely. Less than expected truants returned the questionnaire;

(c) Truants less likely to return questionnaire.
Respondents may not tell the truth.

4 (a) $X^2 = 72.8$ cv 7.815 snoring associated with heart disease;

(b) Snore more e.g. more sufferers snore every night than expected;

(c) No. Heart disease and snoring associated but there is no proof of cause and effect.

5 (a) $X^2 = 33.5$ cv 7.815 outcome not independent of treatment;

(b) New treatment effective since number of those receiving new treatment who show marked improvement greater than expected;

(c)

	Died	Refused	Untraceable
New	19	10	15
Standard	3	12	18

cv 5.99 reason depends on treatment.

(d) New treatment has a high risk of death and so should not be used. This was hidden in first set of data where patients who died were included in the category 'information unobtainable'.

Exam style practice paper

1 (a) 1.44, 0.620;

(b) 0.6;

(c) Regular user would probably make sure they had sufficient change. Their journey probably 80p or £1.20.

2 (a) $t = 2.01$ cv 1.860 applicants take longer than current employees;

(b) $t = 1.37$ cv 1.860 no significant evidence of a difference.

3 (a) 19.1 cv 5.991 views associated with area;

(b) (i) cv 5.991 answer independent of area,
(ii) cv 5.991 answer independent of area;

(c) Appears car users in all areas have similar views as do non-car users in all areas. Difference between areas found in **(a)** could be due to different proportions of car users in different areas.

4 (b) 3.75, 0.968;

  (c) £1.80.

5 (a) 0.027–1.67;

  (b) Normal distribution, random sample;

  (c) Outlier of 3.9 suggests distribution may not be normal;

  (d) 0.87–1.15;

  (e) Large sample hence mean can be assumed to be normally distributed, sample stated to be random;

  (f) 631.

alternative hypothesis 45–**46**
answers to exercises 112–120

χ^2 [chi squared] distribution 85–86
   percentage points table 111
confidence intervals 23–44
   key point summary 43
   normal distribution mean – large
      sample, sample deviation unknown
      29–30–38
   normal distribution mean – standard
      deviation known 23–24–**25**–26–28
   sample mean – standard deviation
      unknown 39–**40**–41–43
contingency tables 83–104
   χ^2 [chi squared] distribution 85–86
   combining classes **93**
   definition **83**
   key point summary 103–104
   small expected values 92–**93**–94–97
   use **83**–**85**–86–92
   Yate's [continuity] correction **98**–100
continuous distribution
   mean **10**–11–15
   standard deviation 10
   variance **10**–11–15
continuous random variable, expected
   value **9**
critical region 47–48–**49**
critical value 49
critical t values 68
critical z values 63

degrees of freedom 39
discrete random variable
   expected value **1**–**2**
   mean **2**–**3**–4–9
   standard deviation 3
   variance **2**–**3**–4–9

errors in testing hypotheses 55–**56**–57–59
examination style practice paper 105–107,
   answers 119–120

hypothesis testing 45–62
   alternative hypothesis 45–**46**
   critical region 47–48–**49**
   critical value 49
   errors 55–**56**–57–59
   forming a hypothesis 45–**46**
   general procedure **49**–50–54
   key point summary 59–60
   null hypothesis 45–**46**
   one-tailed tests 46–**47**, 48, 70, 74–76
   population mean **47**

rejection 49
   sample mean **47**
   significance levels 47–48–**49**, 54–55
   test statistic **47**
   two-tailed tests 46–**47**, 49, 69
   type 1 error 56–58
   type 2 error 56–58
hypothesis testing for means 63–82
   approach to problems 73–76
   critical t values 68
   critical z values 63
   key point summary 80
   large sample, unspecified distribution
      63–64–67
   normal distribution, sample not large,
      standard deviation unknown
      67–**68**–69–72

key point summaries
   confidence intervals 43
   contingency tables 103–104
   hypothesis testing 59–60
   hypothesis testing for means 80
   probability distributions 20–21

large sample, unspecified distribution
   hypothesis test for means **63**–64–67
large, arbitrary definition of 29

normal distribution
   function table 108
   percentage points table 109
normal distribution mean confidence
   limits
   large sample, standard deviation
      unknown **29**–30–38
   standard deviation known
      23–24–**25**–26–28
normal distribution hypothesis test for
   means
   sample not large, standard deviation
      unknown 67–**68**–69–72
notation
   expected value: E(X) 1
   mean of a discrete random
      variable: μ 2
   random variables: particular values
      lower case: x 1
   random variables: upper case X 1
   test statistic X^2: [not universally
      recognised symbol] 85
   variance of a discrete distribution: σ 2
null hypothesis 45–**46**

one-tailed tests 46–**47**, 48, 70, 74–76

population mean, hypothesis **47**
probability distributions 1–22
  continuous distribution – mean
    10–11–15
  continuous distribution – standard
    deviation 10
  continuous distribution – variance
    10–11–15
  continuous random variable – expected
    value **9**
  discrete random variable – expected
    value **1–2**
  discrete random variable – mean
    2–3–4–9
  discrete random variable – standard
    deviation 3
  discrete random variable – variance
    2–3–4–9
  key point summary 20–21
  rectangular distribution **15**–16–18
  uniform distribution 15

random selection, importance 47
rectangular distribution **15**–16–18

rejection of hypothesis 49

sample mean
  hypothesis about population mean **47**
  confidence intervals, standard deviation
    unknown **39–40**–41–43
significance levels 47–48–**49**, 54–55
small expected values 92–**93**–94–97
standard deviation, estimated on past
  experience 41
statistical inference 23
statistical tables 108–111
statistically significant results 45
Student's t distribution 39
  percentage points table 110

t distribution 39
  percentage points table 110
test statistic **47**
two-tailed tests 46–**47**, 49, 69
type 1 error 56–58
type 2 error 56–58

Yate's [continuity] correction **98**–100